North Aleutian Basin Energy-Fisheries

Workshop Proceedings

March 18-19, 2008
Anchorage, Alaska

Brian J. Allee, Editor

AK-SG-09-03
$15.00

Published by Alaska Sea Grant
University of Alaska Fairbanks

North Aleutian Basin Energy-Fisheries Workshop (2008 : Anchorage, Alaska)

North Aleutian Basin energy-fisheries : workshop proceedings, March 18-19, 2008, Anchorage, Alaska / Brian Allee, editor.— Fairbanks : Alaska Sea Grant College Program, University of Alaska Fairbanks, [2009]

   p. : ill. ; cm.—(AK-SG ; 09-03)

   Includes bibliographical references.

ISBN 978-1-56612-137-8

doi:10.4027/nabef.2008

   1. Fisheries—Aleutian Basin—Congresses. 2. Petroleum industry and trade—Environmental aspects—Aleutian Basin—Congresses. I. Allee, Brian James. II. Alaska Sea Grant College Program. III. Title. IV. Series: Alaska Sea Grant College Program report ; 09-03.

SH222.A4 N665 2008

Citation: Allee, B.J. (ed.) 2009. North Aleutian Basin energy-fisheries: Workshop proceedings. Alaska Sea Grant, University of Alaska Fairbanks.

Credits

This book is published by the Alaska Sea Grant College Program, supported by the U.S. Department of Commerce, NOAA National Sea Grant Office, grant NA06OAR4170013, project A/161-01, and by the University of Alaska Fairbanks with state funds. Funding for the publication and workshop was also provided by the Alaska Crab Coalition, Aleutians East Borough, At-sea Processors Association, Bristol Bay Native Corporation, North Pacific Fishery Management Council, Peter Pan Seafoods, Shell Oil Company, United Fishermen of Alaska, and the University of Alaska. The University of Alaska is an affirmative action/equal opportunity employer and educational institution.

Sea Grant is a unique partnership with public and private sectors combining research, education, and technology transfer for public service. This national network of universities meets changing environmental and economic needs of people in our coastal, ocean, and Great Lakes regions.

Cover design and book layout by Jen Gunderson, and editing by Sue Keller, of Alaska Sea Grant.

Alaska Sea Grant College Program
University of Alaska Fairbanks
P.O. Box 755040
Fairbanks, Alaska 99775-5040
Toll free (888) 789-0090
(907) 474-6707   Fax (907) 474-6285
http://www.alaskaseagrant.org

Contents

Panel: Meeting the Environmental Challenge in the North Aleutian Basin

Panel: Concerns and Issues from the Fishing Industry

Panel: Perspectives on Energy-Fisheries Coexistence in Norway

Panel: Oil & Gas Impact

Panel: North Aleutian Basin Potentially Impacted Communities—Opportunities and Concerns

Panel: Native Culture and Subsistence Implications

Panel: Perspectives on Energy-Fisheries in Cook Inlet

Introduction

The North Aleutian Basin Energy-Fisheries Workshop was held March 18-19, 2008, in Anchorage, Alaska. The workshop was open to the public, and about 240 people attended. Brian Allee, director of the Alaska Sea Grant College Program, was master of ceremonies at the workshop. In addition, a smaller workshop on the same topic was held in Kodiak March 20, 2008.

During the North Aleutian Basin Energy-Fisheries Workshop, many valuable discussions took place concerning proposed federal oil and gas lease sales in Alaska's North Aleutian Basin and the potential impact on fisheries and communities. The 2007-2012 Outer Continental Shelf Oil and Gas Proposed Program, developed by the U.S. Department of Interior Minerals Management Service (MMS), calls for North Aleutian Basin Lease Sale 214 to occur in 2011.

This publication is the proceedings of the two-day workshop. To view PowerPoint presentations for most contributions, see http://seagrant.uaf.edu/conferences/2008/energy-fisheries/agenda.html.

Abundant Natural and Energy Resources in the North Aleutian Basin

The North Aleutian Basin is a large geographic area that encompasses the southeastern Bering Sea continental shelf, including all of Bristol Bay. The potential for natural gas and oil makes the basin particularly attractive for exploration. The basin, the Bering Sea, and the 1,500-mile-long Aleutian Island archipelago contain some of the nation's richest and most revered fisheries, marine mammal and seabird habitat, and stunning natural beauty. The region also has essential habitat for endangered species including the North Pacific right whale and Steller sea lion. The abundant natural fisheries resources are the foundation of the region's commercial and subsistence economies and are integral to its people and communities.

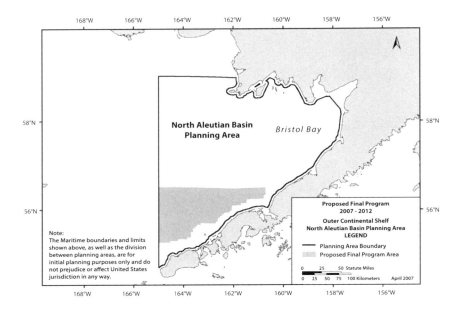

Map showing region and North Aleutian Basin.
Source: U.S. Minerals Management Service.

Facts at a glance

- The North Aleutian Basin is northwest of the Alaska Peninsula. The proposed lease sale area lies 12-200 miles offshore, west of Nelson Lagoon, Port Moller, and Cold Bay.

- The basin is estimated to contain 8.6 trillion cubic feet of gas and 750 million barrels of oil or condensate.

- If developed, the basin's energy resources may be worth $37 billion over the next 30 years.

- Bering Sea fisheries (pollock, cod, sablefish, king crab, Tanner crab, salmon, halibut) are worth approximately $2 billion per year.

- The Bering Sea is home to marine mammals such as seals, Steller sea lions, walrus, and 16 species of whales, including the endangered North Pacific right whale.

- Bristol Bay supports the largest natural sockeye salmon run in the world, which provides thousands of jobs to commercial fishermen and processor workers.

Acknowledgments

The University of Alaska Fairbanks, through the Alaska Sea Grant College Program based at the School of Fisheries and Ocean Sciences, was asked to facilitate the North Aleutian Basin Energy-Fisheries initiative and workshop. Partners include the University of Alaska and Norway's Bodø University. Bodø brings firsthand experience to this effort, having assisted similar collaborations among fisheries and energy interests in Norway. More than twenty-two supporters and/or contributors supported the North Aleutian Basin Energy-Fisheries initiative. More information is available at alaskaseagrant.org.

The North Aleutian Basin Energy-Fisheries Steering Committee organized the workshop. Having generously served its purpose, the committee was dissolved in June 2008. Members were

Kevin Banks, Alaska Department of Natural Resources
Joe Childers, United Fishermen of Alaska
Bubba Cook, World Wildlife Fund
Marilyn Crockett, Alaska Oil & Gas Association
Justine Gundersen, Nelson Lagoon Village
Troy Johnson, Aleut Corporation
Stanley Mack, Mayor, Aleutians East Borough
Stephanie Madsen, At-sea Processors Association
Shirley Marquardt, Mayor, City of Unalaska
Gregg Nady, Shell Exploration and Production Company
Dan O'Hara, Mayor, Bristol Bay Borough
Eric Olson, Chairman, North Pacific Fishery Management Council
Brent Paine, United Catcher Boats
Bill Popp, Anchorage Economic Development Council
Alice Ruby, Mayor, City of Dillingham
Dale Schwarzmiller, Peter Pan Seafoods
Daniel Sharp, Minerals Management Service
Tiel Smith, Bristol Bay Native Corporation
Jan-Oddvar Sørnes, Bodø University
Ken Taylor, Alaska Department of Fish and Game
Arni Thomson, Alaska Crab Coalition
Denis Wiesenburg, Dean, School of Fisheries and Ocean Sciences, University of Alaska Fairbanks

In addition to steering committee members, the following people organized the workshop: David Holt, Bodø University; Bob Juettner, Aleutians East Borough; Ann Ringstad, University of Alaska; and Brian Allee, Sherri Pristash, Sue Keller, and Doug Schneider, Alaska Sea Grant, University of Alaska Fairbanks.

All steering committee members were asked to support the workshop. Financial contributors are gratefully acknowledged:

Alaska Crab Coalition	$1,000
Aleutians East Borough	$5,000
At-sea Processors Association	$5,000
Bristol Bay Native Corporation	$5,000
North Pacific Fishery Management Council	$3,000
Peter Pan Seafoods	$5,000
Shell Oil Company	$25,000
United Fishermen of Alaska	$1,000
University of Alaska	$20,000

Agenda: North Aleutian Basin Energy-Fisheries Workshop

Day 1: March 18, 2008

7:00 – 8:00 am   Registration and coffee

8:00 – 8:15 am   Welcome and Opening Remarks, Announcements, Introductions
Denis Wiesenburg, Dean, School of Fisheries and Ocean Sciences, University of Alaska Fairbanks

8:15 – 8:30 am   Keynote Presentation: Dialogue Is Important
Mark Hamilton, President, University of Alaska

8:30 – 9:00 am   The One Ocean Model: Fishing and Petroleum Industries in Newfoundland and Labrador, Canada
Gordon Slade, Executive Director, One Ocean, Canada

Audience Q & A

9:00 – 9:30 am   Continental Shelf Background
John Goll, Director, Minerals Management Service, Alaska Regional Outer Continental Shelf

Audience Q & A

9:30 – 10:00 am   Offshore Oil and Gas Development Scenario
Gregg Nady, Commercial Team Leader for Alaska Exploration, Shell Exploration and Production Company

Audience Q & A

10:00 – 10:15 am Break

10:15 – 11:15 am Federal Fisheries in the North Aleutian Basin
Jane DiCosimo, Senior Plan Coordinator, North Pacific Fishery Management Council

Coordinated Management
Earl Krygier, Alaska Department of Fish and Game

Audience Q & A

11:15 am – 12 pm   Application of Structured Decision Making to the
Consideration of Multiple Objectives in Fishery
Resource Management
*Graham Long, Compass Resource Management,
Vancouver, Canada*

Audience Q & A

12:00 – 1:15 pm   Lunch

1:15 – 3:00 pm   Panel: Meeting the Environmental Challenge in the
North Aleutian Basin
Moderator: Brian Allee, Director, Alaska Sea Grant
Panel members:
Bubba Cook, World Wildlife Fund
Kelly Harrell, Alaska Marine Conservation Council
John Devens, Prince William Sound Regional Citizens'
Advisory Council
Jon Kurland, Habitat Director, NOAA Fisheries
Bob Murphy, Fisheries Management Biologist, Alaska
Department of Fish and Game

Audience Q & A

3:00 – 3:15   Break

3:15 – 5:00 pm   Panel: Concerns and Issues from the
Fishing Industry
Moderator: Jeff Stephan, United Fishermen's
Marketing Association
Panel members:
Arni Thomson, Alaska Crab Coalition
Brent Paine, United Catcher Boats
Dale Schwarzmiller, Peter Pan Seafoods
Eric Olson, North Pacific Fishery Management Council

Audience Q & A

5:00 – 5:15 pm   Day 1 Wrap-up: Setting the Stage for Day 2

5:30 – 7:00 pm   Reception

Day 2: March 19, 2008

8:00 – 8:05 am   Welcome and Opening Remarks, Announcements

8:05 – 9:05 am   Perspectives on Energy-Fisheries Coexistence
in Norway
Jan Oddvar Sørnes, Bodø University
Jan Terje Henriksen, Bodø University
Hans Nordgård, Bodø University
Per Eidsvik, Nordland County
James Parker, Shell Oil International Exploration
*   and Production*

     Audience Q & A

9:05 – 10:15 am   Presentations and Panel Discussion:
Oil & Gas Impact
Moderator: David Holt, Bodø University, Norway
Jerry Payne, Department of Fisheries and Oceans,
Newfoundland, Canada
Cindi Godsey, Environmental Protection Agency,
*   Alaska Operations*
Dick Prentki, Minerals Management Service Oceanographer

     Audience Q & A

10:15 – 10:30 am   Break

10:30 am – 12 pm   Panel: North Aleutian Basin Potentially Impacted
Communities—Opportunities and Concerns
Moderator: Stephanie Madsen, At-sea Processors
Panel members:
Shirley Marquardt, Mayor, City of Unalaska
Justine Gundersen, Nelson Lagoon Village
Tim Sands, Dillingham City Council
Dan O'Hara, Mayor, Bristol Bay Borough
Glen Alsworth, Mayor, Lake and Peninsula Borough
Stanley Mack, Mayor, Aleutians East Borough

     Audience Q & A

12:00 – 1:30 pm   Lunch

1:30 – 2:45 pm   Panel: Native Culture and Subsistence Implications
Moderator: Eric Olson, North Pacific Fishery
*   Management Council*
Panel members:
Tiel Smith, Bristol Bay Native Corporation
Norman Anderson, Commercial and Subsistence Fisherman
James Fall, ADFG Subsistence Division

Audience Q & A

2:45 – 3:00 pm   Break

3:00 – 4:15 pm   Panel: Perspectives on Energy-Fisheries in Cook Inlet
                   Moderator: Roy Agloinga, Coordinator, Anchorage
                   *   Rural Affairs*
                   Panel members:
                   John Williams, Mayor, Kenai Peninsula Borough
                   Bill Popp, Anchorage Economic Development Corporation
                   Gary Fandrei, Cook Inlet Aquaculture Association
                   Steve Grabacki, GRAYSTAR Pacific Seafood, Ltd.
                   Michael Munger, Cook Inlet Regional Citizens
                   *   Advisory Council*
                   Bob Shavelson, Cook Inletkeeper

                   Audience Q & A

4:15 – 5:15 pm   Audience Decides on Next Steps

                   Informal discussion to answer questions and
                   develop an action plan.

                   1. Topics of most interest to you.
                   2. How best to go forward and expand dialogue.
                       a. Another workshop?
                       b. Community meetings?
                       c. Form regional citizens advisory council?
                       d. Research needs?
                   3. Develop action plan and next steps.

5:15 pm   Closing Remarks

The One Ocean Model: The Fishing and Petroleum Industries in Newfoundland and Labrador

Gordon Slade, Executive Director
One Ocean Corporation, St. John's, Newfoundland, Canada

In the winter of 2002, the regulator for the province's offshore petroleum sector, the Canada-Newfoundland and Labrador Offshore Petroleum Board (C-NLOPB), and the Fisheries and Marine Institute of Memorial University of Newfoundland sponsored a series of meetings with industry representatives from the fishing and petroleum sectors. The objective was the establishment of an inter-industry organization to facilitate and enhance working relationships by promoting mutual understanding of industry operational activities in the marine environment.

These meetings resulted in the formation of One Ocean in the spring of 2002. One Ocean is the liaison organization for the province's fishing and petroleum industries; the model is unique to Canada and the world.

The organization's mandate:

One Ocean shall be the medium for information exchange regarding industry operational activities between the fishing and petroleum industries in Newfoundland and Labrador, and as an informed entity, will initiate research and industry-specific activities to meet industry challenges, as well as promote cooperation, transparency, and information dissemination between these industry sectors.

One Ocean provides a neutral forum for two vital industry sectors to facilitate communication, information exchange, and shared opportunities. This process is based on the initiatives of each industry to endorse cooperation, education and awareness, transparency, and trust between two industries operating in a common marine environment.

The structure of One Ocean

One Ocean is composed of a Secretariat, and Industry Board and its Chairman, and is housed at the Fisheries and Marine Institute of

Memorial University of Newfoundland. The Industry Board consists of equal, knowledgeable, and senior petroleum and fisheries members as well as their affiliate industry regulators as Official Observers. Petroleum representatives on the Industry Board include the Canadian Association of Petroleum Producers (CAPP), Chevron Canada Resources, Hibernia Management and Development Company-ExxonMobil, Husky Energy, Petro-Canada, and StatoilHydro.

Fisheries members include the Fish Food and Allied Workers (FFAW) union and the Association of Seafood Producers. Official Observer status for industry regulators includes the C-NLOPB (petroleum regulator), and the Department of Fisheries and Oceans (DFO) (fisheries regulator). The Canadian Coast Guard (CCG) and Marine Institute are also Official Observers on the Industry Board. Industry Board representatives sit face-to-face to discuss operational activity issues, as well as government mandates and legislative frameworks. One Ocean is not directed by government mandates but by mutual recognition of both industries to promote understanding and awareness of industry operational activities.

The One Ocean model enables a proactive approach to potential areas of conflict between the fishing and petroleum sectors before they become problematic. It is the responsibility of the One Ocean Secretariat to identify these concerns and provide comprehensive analyses to each industry. The Secretariat continually updates its research and literature reviews on a regional and international basis and covers the groundwork necessary to provide relevant information on potential effects for each operational sector.

The Secretariat assists in organizing and actively participates in consultations between the petroleum and fishing industries. During these consultations, One Ocean ensures that petroleum proponents have current and relevant fisheries data in areas where oil and gas activity is proposed. This enables meaningful discussion on temporal and spatial components as fisheries representatives are consulted on when and where the proposed oil and gas activity occurs.

These consultations include proposed 2-D and 3-D seismic surveys, electromagnetic surveys, drilling programs, glory holes, and tow-outs— essentially all proposed petroleum-related activities. As a result of these meetings, fishers in the province have become very familiar with the existing production fields and the associated activities involved in exploration. From the petroleum side, there is a much better understanding of where harvesters fish and when, the type of vessels and gear used, and the species caught. Proponents also engage FFAW fishers as Fisheries Liaison Observers (FLO) to monitor activity on board seismic vessels during seismic collection.

Why do Newfoundland and Labrador need One Ocean?

The island of Newfoundland is 113,390 km² and mainland Labrador is 291,330 km², giving us a coastline that expands over 17,542 km. Although the province has a vast geographic area, the population is approximately 506,000. Of the 694 communities in Newfoundland and Labrador, 608 are coastal communities (2 km radius).

The last province to join Canada, in 1949, the island of Newfoundland and Labrador brought to Canada its unique system of values associated with its marine environment. The province is a major contributor to Canada's longest coastline in the world and second largest continental shelf.

It was the fishery that lured settlers to the island of Newfoundland more than 500 years ago, and it is the diverse evolution of the fishery that has defined us socially, culturally, and economically. The collapse of the groundfish fishery in the early 1990s devastated the entire rural coastal economy of Newfoundland, directly affecting the livelihood of 30,000 fishermen and plant workers and eliminating the economic mainstay of 510 communities. Although harvesters experienced a transition from groundfish to shellfish that proved economically viable, the societal catastrophe is still felt today. During this period of economic and social imparity brought about as a result of a declining and unprecedented structural adjustment in the fishery, the prospect of a lucrative petroleum industry offshore Newfoundland and Labrador instilled a belief of economic recovery and even prosperity.

The Newfoundland and Labrador offshore petroleum industry is a relative newcomer—approximately 35 years young. There are currently three production fields producing approximately 420,000 barrels per day, with an average annual production value of $8 billion. The Hibernia Gravity Based Structure (GBS), the province's first producing field, began production in 1997. The second field, the Terra-Nova, uses a floating production storage and offloading (FPSO) vessel and had its first oil in 2002. The third field, White Rose, also uses an FPSO, *Sea Rose,* and began production in 2005.

In the same vicinity as the three production fields, about 300 km from St. John's, Newfoundland, in a region called the Grand Banks, 40% or 20,000 metric tons (t) of crab, is harvested, the province's most valued fishery resource. These traditional stomping grounds are now shared with oil rigs, tankers, supply ships, and seismic vessels.

The C-NLOPB marine jurisdiction covers 1,825,992 km². There are currently 32 active exploration licenses in the Grand Banks region and the next potential development is the Hebron field with 581 million barrels of heavy oil. No start-up date has been announced. Other potential future developments include natural gas—the offshore area has an estimated 7 trillion cubic feet of natural gas. The C-NLOPB is offering four land parcels in offshore Labrador; it is speculated that interest is in natural gas development. Call for bids on these parcels closes in August 2008.

One Ocean initiatives and activities

Since 2002, One Ocean has endeavored to identify priorities and areas of interest mutually beneficial to the petroleum and fishing sectors. As a result of the One Ocean Industry Workshop in 2003, seismic survey and oil spill preparedness and response have been the focus of the Secretariat.

One Ocean held a Seismic Information Session in 2004, and cosponsored a Seismic Workshop in 2006 for fishing and petroleum representatives, government departments and agencies, and academia. One Ocean has actively participated in technical advisory groups and participated in and presented at conferences regarding research on the potential impacts of seismic surveys on fish and fish habitat in the province and on an international level.

Oil spill preparedness and response:
Environmental emergency oil spill card

One Ocean's research on oil spill preparedness and response capability in the province has led to several collaborative projects with provincial and federal government departments, industry, academia, and communities. In 2004 the Marine Environmental Emergency Oil Spill Information Card was produced and distributed to over 5,000 fishers. It provides detailed information on identifying a spill, what to do as a mitigative measure, and whom to contact, and provides a 24-hour emergency number. The card is printed on waterproof, adhesive material suitable for marine vessels. Since 2004 the card has been distributed to all tankers docking at the transshipment terminal and oil refinery in the province and will be circulated to tourism operators and recreational marine users this year.

Oil spill preparedness and response:
Training of fishers in oil spill countermeasures

The most important project One Ocean has undertaken is to train 500 fisheries workers in oil spill countermeasures in the onshore and nearshore interface. Industry and government partners in this project have developed a five-day training program that will take place in 15 communities throughout Newfoundland and Labrador. The curriculum/ fieldwork for the course was developed to meet and surpass international standards and is a certified program. The Fisheries and Marine Institute provide instructors for the in situ community training with the $600,000 mobile trailer designed and built specifically for this course. Government departments have committed to actively participate in the program for its entirety and fisheries groups endorse and promote the program.

The major objective of this project is to enhance understanding of oil spill response at a community level. Providing community-based oil spill countermeasure training will ensure faster response time. Timing is critical in terms of mitigating the impact of oil contamination on shorelines, marine species, habitat, seabirds, and waterfowl. The training of fisheries workers in oil spill countermeasures is a logical and cost-effective practice. Fishers have an inherent knowledge of the geophysical and biophysical components of the ocean. It also provides a new awareness and understanding of the oil and gas sector that operates in the same marine environment.

Oil spill preparedness and response: An environmental emergency plan for North Harbour

One Ocean, students from the Fisheries and Marine Institute, industry, and government representatives recognized the need for community-based preparedness in the event of an environmental emergency. The town of North Harbour, Placentia Bay, was chosen as the pilot community as it is located within the busiest region of hydrocarbon transshipment in Canada.

The question posed to the community was, Is North Harbour prepared for an environmental emergency?

The project is based on the need to prioritize proactive versus reactive practices at the community level. Partners in the project organized community meetings and distributed a questionnaire to assist in the development of an emergency plan. The questionnaire enabled students to determine the socioeconomic risks associated with the area, inventory of the community and surrounding area, demographic components, population, and other critical logistical information.

Students conducted on-site fieldwork, developed a GIS mapping system of the area including "sensitive" areas, and developed a document listing organizations involved in response and contact information, highlighting personal preparedness, community rights, and recommendations to assist the community in preparing and updating its environmental emergency plan. This plan template can be used by other communities throughout the province to develop community-specific emergency plans.

Study tours 2002 and 2008

One Ocean initiatives also include two study tours to Scotland and Norway (2002 and 2008). The purpose of the study tours was to explore how similar inter-industry groups in other parts of the world operate, with the hope of taking lessons learned from these jurisdictions and implementing them into the functioning of the One Ocean organization.

One Ocean Ottawa Delegation

Since 2005, One Ocean has organized the One Ocean Ottawa Delegation. Representatives from the One Ocean Industry Board and Secretariat travel to Ottawa, parliamentary capital of Canada, to meet with federal ministers and their departments to update them on One Ocean activities. The One Ocean model provides the opportunity for the petroleum and fishing sectors to meet with government departments and agencies as a single entity to discuss issues of mutual interest.

Canada Ocean Lecture Series

In 2006 One Ocean cosponsored the first Canada Ocean Lecture Series. The lecture series is a Canadian initiative—with specific focus on Canadian issues; however, it is global in scope and participation, reflecting a comprehensive and encompassing venue for discussion and review.

The lecture series takes place annually in Canada, in conjunction with an international symposium or assembly of ocean practitioners, managers, analysts, scientists, government leaders, and/or stakeholders. The general public is invited to attend the lecture. Each series has a specific topic related to ocean development as well as an action plan, with the results announced and discussed at the following lecture.

In 2006, the inaugural Canada Ocean Lecture Series took place in St. John's, Newfoundland and Labrador. The Honorable John Fraser presented "Who Speaks for the Oceans and What Are They Doing about It?" The 2007 series was in Ottawa, where Dr. Eddy Carmack presented "Climate, Resources and Human Issues Affecting the Arctic Oceans Today."

It is vital that all ocean users are cognizant of operational activities in the offshore areas to ensure sustainable use and protection of the marine environment and promote industry cooperation. Since 2002, One Ocean has been a progressive advocate for sustainable coexistence of the Newfoundland and Labrador fishing and petroleum industries. This model can be extrapolated into any region where marine industries must coexist.

One Ocean will continue to provide a neutral forum for the fishing and petroleum industries in Newfoundland and Labrador. The success of this model to exist as a proactive entity that facilitates the opportunity for information dissemination and progressive joint initiatives for two sectors operating in one ocean has proven mutually beneficial to the industries that created it.

Questions and answers

Q: How is oil transported from the platforms offshore to wherever else it may go; is it transported via pipeline or tanker?

GORDON SLADE: The oil is transported with tankers. Some tankers carry 850,000 barrels from the rigs into the location where there's a storage area. Then it is transported with smaller tankers to the markets in the United States.

Q: Can you talk to us about the recent Labrador Land Claims? How might that impact, or has it already impacted, the fishing industry and the oil and gas industry?

GORDON SLADE: There is no real involvement between One Ocean and local governments other than when the consultations take place between the oil industry and the fishing industry. Local governments are involved because a lot of the people go out to the community level and chambers of commerce and anyone who wants to sit in on the consultations can do so. In terms of Labrador the aboriginal people, the Inuit in particular, have certain rights for their new territory, Newhasenvuit. If oil and gas were to be developed in that area, a very specific set of consultations needs to take place.

Q: Thank you. Who makes the decisions regarding operational procedures, legislative issues, and regulations in the Newfoundland organizations?

GORDON SLADE: The decisions about operational issues are made right there in a meeting. Here's an example. A massive piece of equipment, called a spider, had to be towed out of the Terra Nova field to the Terra Nova rig because it could have caused damage to crab fishermen's gear. All of that was coordinated from One Ocean. A group of people were assigned to figure out how to tow the spider in a way that did not have any impact on the fishermen's gear.

Q: What have been the major impacts that you have encountered in the development in that area? I understand you have the largest tides in the world in that particular region of Canada.

GORDON SLADE: New Brunswick has tides that are much greater than Newfoundland. It's very important to keep ahead of what's going on so there are no surprises. The secret to this is being able to inform the fishers as to what is coming down the road. You must anticipate what might be a problem and deal with it in advance. We haven't run into any significant problems at the operational level to date. And that's since 2002.

The Outer Continental Shelf Program

John Goll, Regional Director–Alaska

U.S. Minerals Management Service, Anchorage, Alaska

The U.S. Minerals Management Service is an ocean, energy, and mineral agency within the U.S. Department of the Interior. MMS manages the seabed of the outer continental shelf (OCS) of the United States—generally the area three miles and beyond from the coast. About 1 billion acres exist off Alaska.

MMS oversees all phases of activity—leasing, regulation, monitoring, and inspection of industry activity. Commodities include oil, natural gas, sulfur, sand, gravel, gold, and other minerals. Recently MMS was given the responsibility for alternative energy on the OCS, which includes wind, ocean currents, waves, solar, and tides. MMS also collects and distributes royalties from all federal and Indian lands, onshore and offshore, which has been about $5-10 billion in recent years. To support its regulatory role, MMS sponsors both environmental and technical research.

To accomplish such a broad mission, MMS has a diverse group of employees, ranging from engineers, geologists, geophysicists, to marine biologists, oceanographers, meteorologists, archaeologists, sociologists, economists, and more.

The Outer Continental Shelf Lands Act with its Amendments is the overarching law that provides the legal framework for OCS activity. In addition to the OCSLA, MMS and industry must follow other relevant U.S. laws that are governed by other agencies. These include the National Environmental Policy Act, the Clean Air and Clean Water Acts, the Endangered Species Act, the Marine Mammal Protection Act, the National Historic Preservation Act, the Oil Pollution Act, the Coastal Zone Management Act, plus more. Agencies frequently involved include the U.S. Coast Guard, the Environmental Protection Agency, the National Oceanic and Atmospheric Administration, the Fish and Wildlife Service, and the Corps of Engineers. The State of Alaska, local boroughs, and local tribal governments may regulate certain aspects of activity or be consulted.

The OCS decision-making process has been described as pyramidal in structure, proceeding from broad-based planning to an increasingly narrower focus as actual development grows more imminent. The 5 Year Program looks widely nationwide, while ultimately a development facility may cover only a very small part of the seabed, on the order of acres. Likewise information becomes more specific as the phases progress. MMS geologists will estimate the potential for oil and natural gas for the planning areas that subdivide the nation's OCS. As companies explore and develop, they will key information for the site of the activity, and eventually cull out areas that have poorer potential.

Every five years, MMS sets up a schedule of sales after a review and consultation with the coastal states. For any potential sale on the 5 Year Program, MMS will complete another full evaluation to assess whether the sale should be held, and if so, over what area and with what conditions.

For the current 5 Year Program which covers 2007-2012, MMS announced four areas for potential sales off Alaska:

- Beaufort Sea—two sales (2009, 2011) but without areas used for subsistence whaling near Barrow and Kaktovik.

- Chukchi Sea—three sales (2008, 2010, 2012) with a minimum 25-mile buffer zone to defer the nearshore corridor used in the spring migration northward for whales, seals, birds, and other fauna.

- Bering Sea—one sale (2011) in the North Aleutian Basin, but limited to the southwest portion of the planning area.

- Cook Inlet—the possibility of two sales, but only if sufficient interest is expressed.

The State of Alaska holds annual sales in State waters of the Beaufort Sea and Cook Inlet.

The process to evaluate a sale includes preparation of an environmental evaluation, plus seeking public information and comment at several steps. Before a final decision is made on a sale, the MMS will seek the recommendations from the governor of Alaska on the size, timing, and location of the sale. The OCSLA gives strong deference to the views of the governor. If a decision is made to proceed with the sale, MMS will publish a notice explaining the terms of the sale, plus any additional operational requirements that companies must follow (in addition to those requirements already in place in MMS and other agencies' rules.) Bids are taken competitively, and afterward MMS will evaluate the bids to ensure that they represented a fair market value. A lease gives a company exclusive right to explore, develop, and produce from that lease, but only if it meets all the requirements set in the lease and in the relevant laws and rules.

If a company decides to explore, or later develop, each phase also undergoes a technical and environmental review, with public notice, and recommendations sought from the State. Companies must ensure that their activities are consistent with the Alaska Coastal Zone Management Plan.

MMS has a robust regulatory program to overview all of industry activity. A key part of the review ensures that the companies will follow the MMS regulations designed to prevent pollution. The MMS rules provide for special measures to ensure that activity will be done safely with consideration for shallow hazards, well design, redundant well control equipment and measures, mandatory subsurface safety valves, and emergency plans for adverse weather and ice and for oil spill response. Third party reviews may be done to evaluate the integrity of the platform from which drilling or production may occur. MMS will assess all safety systems, and will inspect the operation before key activities occur.

MMS is a lead reviewer and regulator for offshore oil spill contingency plans, and will ensure that companies have sufficient techniques and procedures in place to address potential spills. MMS coordinates with the Coast Guard and the State for both routine and surprise drills for spill response.

MMS has strong and long-lived research programs both for technical and environmental issues. The MMS Technology and Assessment Program helps fund various engineering and spill response research. Over the past 25 years, the MMS Environmental Studies Program has funded environmental research in Alaska, to the tune of about $300 million. MMS funds research with universities, other agencies, the private sector, and even jointly with other countries. This allows MMS to go to the best researcher on a topic. In Alaska over the past 15 years, MMS has had a special relationship with the University of Alaska Fairbanks through its Coastal Marine Institute.

For the North Aleutian Basin (Bristol Bay), MMS held a workshop in November 2006 to set up a research agenda for the area. More than 100 scientists, resource managers, and stakeholders attended to discuss topics on physical oceanography, subsistence, sociology, fisheries, marine mammals, and more. In 2007, MMS began a four-year study on the Pacific right whale, with NOAA's National Marine Mammal Laboratory. Likewise, work began on an oceanic circulation model to adapt an existing ice-ocean circulation model of the Bering Sea and Gulf of Alaska to the specific oceanographic conditions within Alaska's Bristol Bay. Upcoming research will include subsistence, juvenile and maturing salmon, and mapping of fish and crab, plus more in future years.

History of prior exploration activity in the North Aleutian Basin

Industry collected a lot of seismic data to prepare for the first lease sale in 1988. One stratigraphic test well (COST well) was drilled with industry funding in 1983. Little or no offshore petroleum activity has occurred in the past 20 years. Geologic studies have been held onshore, and the State of Alaska held two lease sales in the past five years.

Based on the available information, in 2006 MMS published its Oil and Natural Gas Assessment for the OCS. MMS geologists concluded that the North Aleutian Basin area is natural gas prone (more likely gas fields with smaller associated oil resources). The assessment estimated 8.6 trillion cubic feet for natural gas (mean risked technically recoverable) in the planning area, and 750 million barrels of oil (mean risked technically recoverable). Technically recoverable estimates are for all oil and gas that might be present. These volumes do not consider any of the commercial aspects, such as market prices, available leases, funding for exploration drilling, and discovery success rates.

The area in which companies bid in Sale 92 in the late 1980s appears to be a gas-prone geologic play, perhaps comparable to Cook Inlet. Onshore areas and offshore areas to the southwest could be more oil-prone.

For further and up-to-date information on the MMS regulatory program, technical and environmental research, geologic data, or the status of the North Aleutian Basin sale process, please check the MMS Alaska Region Web site at www.mms.gov/alaska.

Questions and answers

Q: You mentioned the governor plays a big role in this. Why aren't federally recognized tribes being consulted?

JOHN GOLL: Under the Outer Continental Shelf Lands Act, deference is given to the governor of the affected state. We do consult with the tribes through the sale process. That information is passed on to the decision makers in Washington, D.C. The Secretary of the Interior ultimately makes decisions on the sale.

Q: You mentioned a number of entities that the Minerals Management Service is going to consult with in this process. Is the North Pacific Fishery Management Council one of those entities?

JOHN GOLL: It can be, yes. I just identified the major groups who would be consulted. When we go through scoping we try to identify all the major groups that can give us the information that we need.

Q: For this oil and gas lease sale, would the environmental impact statement (EIS) be crucial for setting up any future exploration or development that occurs?

JOHN GOLL: Yes. A sale EIS is for evaluating the size and location of a sale, plus we look at exploration. We also look at development, but as you notice, the Outer Continental Shelf Lands Act speaks to the phasing of the activity when more is known about where the leases actually are. We would expect to do an environmental impact statement at the development phase.

Q: Are there any circumstances under which you might do a full environmental impact statement to evaluate exploration?

JOHN GOLL: We try to take a good look at the exploration in general through these sale EISs. But the answer to your question would be yes, when you do an environmental assessment one of the questions you're asking is, do you need to do EIS. And so we do evaluate it at that time.

Q: What was the result of the North Pacific right whale study done this summer in the area?

JOHN GOLL: As I understand it, the study was conducted on a vessel and they did not see any right whales. Next year the study will be continued with the National Marine Fisheries Service. Aircraft will be used instead of vessels for better coverage.

Q: Thank you for being here, Mr. Goll. It's good to see you. What is your view of the concept of communication in this process? The MMS process is very formal. When you receive input, parties carefully calculate what their position is and they put it before you and then you decide among the various positions. How do you view the concept of One Ocean? Would it be useful to have an organization that was designed for communication whereby all the interests represented in this room could sit down on a regular basis and actually work out challenges? Then when your formal process occurred, a single message could be communicated.

JOHN GOLL: We mainly want to follow our regulations and the laws and regulations of other agencies. If a process like that was set up where issues were taken care of in advance, and then presented to us, and met the laws that are on the books, it could work.

Offshore Oil and Gas Development Scenario

Gregg Nady, Alaska Exploration Team Leader
Shell Exploration and Production Company, Houston, Texas

I was asked to talk about some development scenarios. It seems in some ways a little bit premature to talk about development scenarios because a lot of decisions have to be made before we get to development. At this time we don't know if there's going to be a lease sale.

I do believe that understanding what a development might look like certainly helps to inform the decision. The more people know about what it might look like, the better-prepared people are. Shared information is certainly helpful.

I have in my hands a 775-page report that Shell prepared back in 1987 before Lease Sale 92, an engineering study that we went through to determine what kind of development system we would put in place in the North Aleutian Basin. My job is to go through this 775-page report in 20 minutes. Actually I won't go through all this, but it is just to let you know that whenever we're looking at a potential development or a lease sale, we take it very seriously and do a lot of engineering studies. We make all of that information available if we end up proposing a development.

I've had a lot of questions from people about ice conditions over the three years that I've been involved in the North Aleutian Basin. There has been some ice in the potential lease sale area for two out of the last eight years. To get information about wave conditions that we might see in the North Aleutian Basin, some information from the North Sea can be applied.

I want to start with a disclaimer. MMS (Minerals Management Service) did a resource assessment in 2006 that indicated the North Aleutian Basin is mostly natural gas—about two-thirds of the resource is expected to be gas, and one-third oil. One thing that we know for sure is that this is not correct! Whatever we find out there is going to be different. We may not find anything. I'm going to talk about some development concepts, and we don't know if there's any oil and gas out here.

A basin just to the west of the North Aleutian Basin, called the St. George Basin, was leased back in the early 1980s. We drilled 10 exploration wells and we didn't find anything there, so the North Aleutian Basin could be the same. On the other hand, Cook Inlet is an example of a place where we did find some oil and gas.

My gut feeling is that there is about a 10-20% chance that enough oil and gas would be discovered to justify development. So number one, you have to find something. Number two, you have to find something big enough to develop. And number three, you've got to go through a new environmental impact study and NEPA process to determine if that kind of development is workable.

Before we get to development we've got to go through a lot of other steps. First, a decision is made whether to have a lease sale, and then a government lease sale is held. Next would be the possibility to get more seismic data. Some two-dimensional seismic data have been taken in the area. Over the last 20 years we've developed another process called three-dimensional seismic, which gives you a three-dimensional picture of the subsurface. That is something that someone might want to do. It's not required but it may be preferable. And then we'll try to find a viable drilling prospect.

We would acquire shallow hazard surveys. That's sort of like a shallow seismic survey to look for shallow gas deposits that can be potentially high pressure, and could cause a well blowout. We would look for seabed impediments, such as shipwrecks, to make sure we wouldn't put the rig on a location that could cause some problems.

We'd file for a drilling permit including our oil spill response plan. That is the time when MMS would do the environmental assessment. And the next phase would be to drill some exploration wells. If we find something, then we drill more wells to find out how big the field is and see if it's big enough to develop. Then we would go through another NEPA process. When could that possibly happen? If there's a lease sale, we could potentially drill wells somewhere between 2012 and 2014.

In St. George Basin we drilled 10 wells. There were four different rigs. They could have used three rigs, but four different companies brought four rigs, so it took nine months to drill 10 exploration wells in the St. George Basin. And we didn't find anything; there's no industry interest to go back there.

There are a couple of other basins. In the Navarin Basin on the border with Russia we drilled nine wells in six months, and didn't find anything. In the Norton Basin we drilled six wells in four months and didn't find anything. So in the North Aleutian Basin, again, it's not guaranteed that we're going to find anything. The time that it takes to determine if there's any oil and/or gas is relatively short. When you consider all the discussion, the debate we're going to go through, it's all going to lead up to a fairly short window of activity to find out if there's any oil or gas.

There are fisheries resources in the North Aleutian Basin, and North Pacific right whale critical habitat. As John Goll said, in the proposed lease sale area only one well has been drilled—a Continental Offshore Stratigraphic Test (COST) well. Twenty-three 3 × 3 mile square leases were issued back in 1988.

MMS did an environmental impact study back in 1984 and it is on their Web site. I looked at a lot of development concepts in that study, and it's a pretty interesting document to go back and read. The basic concept was that if oil or gas were found, there would be a pipeline over the peninsula. There are some better-sheltered deepwater ports on the southeast side of the peninsula, and from there the gas or the oil would be shipped out.

I want to spend a couple of minutes explaining some technology that the oil and gas industry has developed over the last 30 years, and things we do differently now that help us to have an excellent environmental track record. There has not been a significant oil spill from an exploration well in the history of the federal OCS in the United States since 1954. The biggest spill we've had from an exploration well was 200 barrels, in the Gulf of Mexico.

We do shallow seismic hazard surveys, to make sure there aren't any impediments before we put a rig on location. We use pore pressure prediction technology so we can actually look at the seismic data. Based on the velocities of the seismic wave as it bounces off the rock formations we can predict where there's going to be a high-pressure zone. That technology is something that we've developed over the last 30 years. It gives us a better sense of how to design the well to make it safe—to make sure we don't have a well blowout.

Using previous well information is another thing that helps us predict what those bottom hole pressures would be. From the COST well that was drilled in the North Aleutian Basin we can derive information to determine what kind of pressures we might be drilling into.

Before we drill a well we go through a process called "drilling wells on paper," where we get the geology, engineering, operations team together in a room to determine if there are any potential risks. We can design the well to address those risks.

We also have real-time bottom hole pressure monitoring; we call it "measurement while drilling." There's actually a sensor on the drill bit, so we know in real time what the pressures are at the bottom of the well and that helps us react, for example to increase the drilling mud weight to hold back any pressure on the well bore. That information is transmitted within milliseconds at the rig floor where people are operating, but we also have a duplicate operation center in Houston and other locations around the world. We have drilling engineers in these centers, 24 hours a day, seven days a week, monitoring all the wells that we drill. In Alaska, MMS also has an inspector on each drilling rig 24 hours a day, seven days a week.

We also have more benign drilling muds. This is something you put in the well bore to counterbalance the formation pressure, and it also circulates the rock cuttings out of the hole. Now we generally only use water-base mud for exploration wells.

If there is some kind of an event, we have more robust blowout preventers. The typical blowout preventer has four different devices on it that can close a well bore if there's any kind of an adverse pressure event in a well. The ones that we're actually planning to use in Alaska have six devices, so they either close in around the drill pipe or they can actually shear the drill pipe and close the well in completely.

In addition, we'll have a significant oil spill response fleet. For the North Slope we have about $100 million invested in oil spill response equipment, some new vessels, and a spill response barge, etc., just in case.

Platform: A platform has the top side visible above the water. This contains the drilling rig, crew quarters, a heli-deck, some processing equipment, and power generation. We generally try to use the natural gas that we produce in a field to generate the power for the platform. Cranes are required because almost everything that we deliver to the platform comes out on a boat and is lifted onto the platform with a crane. For the North Aleutian Basin a steel jacket would be below the water level, with legs on the order of 10 to 25 feet in diameter, so they are pretty robust. It is held to the seafloor by pilings about seven or eight feet in diameter that are driven from 100 to 300 feet into the seabed to hold the platform in place. The total structure weighs about 40,000 tons.

Wells: The likely design in the North Aleutian Basin would have the well bores inside the legs of the platform. If ice were moving around in the area, which it does occasionally, the well bore would be protected because it's within a 20 foot diameter steel leg of the platform.

The wells are below the seabed, from 5 to 30 wells on each platform. The wells would be deviated. You drill straight down and then "kick" the wells out up to six to eight miles, for one platform. Typically gas fields have fewer wells than the oil fields.

Another option to be considered is a concrete tower, something that's used quite a bit in the North Sea. The well bore goes down the middle of a concrete tower, to protect it from ice, and the wells deviate out from there.

Another technology that's been developed over the last 30 years is called subsea development. An example of that in the Gulf of Mexico is called Nakika. It's a floating platform, so it's buoyant. Six or seven fields are developed by subsea wellhead (the wellhead equipment sits on the seafloor), and flow lines come back to the main platform. This requires steel in the water.

Assuming the mean resource estimate from MMS for the North Aleutian Basin, on the Bering Sea side, you would likely have three to six platforms, depending on how much you found. A pipeline would go over the peninsula. If it's gas most likely a liquefied natural gas plant would be built, where the gas is cooled down to about minus 100 degrees centigrade, to become a liquid. It would be put on a tanker, possibly two or four tankers a month based on the resource MMS projects.

Every liquefied natural gas ship that's built today, of course, is a double hulled tanker. There have been 35,000 cargos of LNG shipped around the world for some 39 years and there's never been a cargo spill. The LNG industry actually originated here in Alaska, in Cook Inlet in 1969. LNG has been safely stored in a lot of places that have seismic activity, e.g., in Japan.

There are some side benefits of the infrastructure, potentially. Some of the vessels we would have to support our efforts would have capabilities to tow stranded boats. About 3,000 ships go through Unimak Pass on the Great Circle Route between the Pacific Northwest and Asia. Annually there would be improved spill response capability and search and rescue. In fact, in the last year or two we have actually gone out to rescue local citizens, enabled by the operations we have in different places. In Canada where we were working on a rig, we rescued a 25 year old guy who was out walking in the wilderness. Also, a family near Barrow was rescued by our search and rescue helicopter.

Regarding personnel, about 250 employees would be needed to run a typical LNG plant, and about 100-150 people would be needed continuously to run a platform.

Questions and answers

Q: The North Aleutian Basin is often described as primarily a gas prospect. What's the likelihood that you would just produce the gas?

GREGG NADY: Most reservoirs have a mixture of some liquids and some natural gas. It wouldn't be all one or the other. MMS wants to go through the safest part of the process first which is exploration and appraisal. And once you actually understand what you have there, then you can design a development system for whatever you find. There will be another environmental impact statement for the development, and the public can have that debate then.

Q: When the initial surveys were done, including the test wells, they did biological assessment in some of those areas. Where are the records kept?

GREGG NADY: Probably MMS is the repository. Over the history of the Alaska OCS, they've spent about $250 million doing environmental studies. To the extent they did studies out here in the past they should have access to the reports.

For Lease Sale 92, MMS included in their lease sale stipulations to have a biological task force. A group of organizations would be represented on the task force, and if there were any activity this task force would be consulted, sort of like a One Ocean.

JOHN GOLL: At MMS we do keep copies of all our research, so things that were done get sent to our office. Contact Dr. Cleve Cowles. We do keep all the vast work that we've done, and we make it available.

Q: Shell and the oil industry want to become good stewards and hire and train people to develop the infrastructure. Can you comment please?

GREGG NADY: For our Beaufort Sea drilling program we hired and trained about 700 people last year. We had over 100 people just working on oil spill response. We used a training center in Kenai for helicopter underwater evacuation training and other kinds of training. We also have people training in the Gulf of Mexico. I was out on a platform a couple of weeks ago and a guy was there from Barrow, Alaska, who was training on a platform to hopefully some day have a job in Alaska.

Q: Where do you envision the platforms being built? Would any work be done in Alaska—in Anchorage or the Ketchikan shipyards, for example?

GREGG NADY: We haven't gotten that far yet. In the previous study, in the 1980s, I'm not sure Anchorage had the capability, but in the Pacific Northwest, the Seattle-Tacoma area has the capability. Everywhere from there to San Francisco to Asia, Korea, were all considered back then. We'd have to look again, today, at the current capabilities in Anchorage and other Alaska sites.

Q: Back in the 1980s MMS did studies in environmental areas, and also in a program called Social and Economic Study Program, SESP. They were a series of studies that had to do with the impact on the commercial fishing industry. The SESP commercial fishing studies should still be in the MMS library.

RESPONSE: Dee Williams is the new environmental studies chief at MMS. One way to find those reports is to call him.

Improving Understanding of Commercial Fisheries in the North Aleutian Basin

Jane DiCosimo, Senior Plan Coordinator
North Pacific Fishery Management Council, Anchorage, Alaska

Earl Krygier, Extended Jurisdiction Program Manager
Alaska Department of Fish and Game, Anchorage, Alaska

Alaska Sea Grant has described the North Aleutian Basin, the nearby Bering Sea, and the 1,500-mile-long Aleutian Island archipelago as containing some of the nation's richest crab, pollock, cod, halibut, and salmon fisheries situated in a healthy ecosystem that provides habitat for vast populations of seabirds and marine mammals. These fisheries are recognized as the best-managed sustainable fisheries in the world. This occurs because they are conservatively managed for stock health and productivity and the management entities have ensured that habitat for spawning, rearing, and growth is maintained. State and federal agencies, along with stakeholders that include coastal communities, environmentalists, and the fishing and associated support industry, invest hundreds of person hours annually and millions of dollars to assess stocks and conduct a transparent public process to modify and develop innovative fishery management measures that insure sustainability and economic health to the region and the Pacific Northwest. This region also is considered essential habitat for species listed under the Endangered Species Act, including the North Pacific right whale, western population of sea otters, Steller sea lions, and short-tailed albatross. The critical habitat of these ESA-listed species can impact the direct and support activities of fisheries as well as any new industries to the area. The abundant natural fisheries resources are the foundation of the region's commercial and subsistence economies and are integral to the fabric and lifestyle of its people and communities[1]. The value to the economies of Alaska, Washington, and Oregon is in the billions of dollars and thousands of jobs in direct fishery participation and support operations for the commercial, sport, and subsistence fisheries. Unknown potential impacts of oil and gas developments in proximity to these fisheries has resulted in an exchange of information between the respective resource users and the state and federal agencies that manage those resources. This workshop is just a part of that exchange.

Valuable commercial groundfish and shellfish fisheries overlap with a proposed North Aleutian Basin oil and gas lease sale, and because of the oceanographic currents that move across this area, any impacts from oil and gas will expand over all of the fishery production area of the eastern Bering Sea.

Because fish do not recognize the limits of state management at 3 nautical miles (nm), marine groundfish and shellfish are managed under cooperative state/federal management through the coordinated efforts of the Alaska Board of Fisheries (Board) and the North Pacific Fishery Management Council (Council). The Magnuson Fishery Conservation and Management Act of 1976 authorized the Council to manage groundfish and shellfish fisheries in the Exclusive Economic Zone (3-200 miles). The Council shares responsibilities with the International Pacific Halibut Commission for Pacific Halibut from 0 to 200 miles. The halibut and sablefish fisheries have been managed under a quota share program since 1995. The fishery management plans (FMP) for groundfish in the Bering Sea and Aleutian Islands (BSAI) includes Pacific cod, walleye pollock, flatfish species, rockfish species, Atka mackerel, sablefish, and incidentally caught species. A moratorium on entry to all groundfish fisheries was implemented in 1995, followed by a strict license limitation program approved in 1998. The Bering Sea pollock fisheries have operated under a fishery cooperative system since 1999, with the passage and subsequent implementation of the American Fisheries Act. Atka mackerel, Pacific ocean perch, and three flatfish species also are managed under a quota share system, which can be fished within a cooperative.

Groundfish harvests in the North Aleutian Basin total 558 million pounds, with an ex-vessel value of nearly $100 million, and comprise approximately 15% of total BSAI groundfish harvests in 2007. Significant overlap occurs between the proposed oil and lease sale in the North Aleutian Basin and prime groundfish fisheries (Fig. 1).

The Board and Council share management responsibilities for crabs, scallops, and salmon. The Fishery Management Plans for BSAI king and Tanner crabs and for scallops outline shared responsibili-

---

[1] As described in the introduction to the workshop at http://seagrant.uaf.edu/conferences/2008/energy-fisheries/info.html#intro.

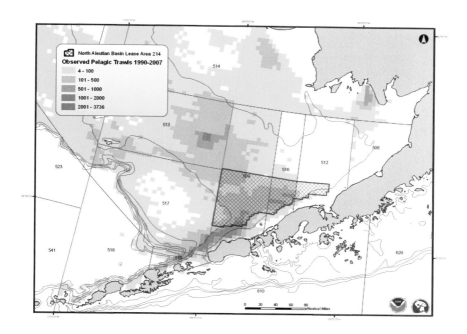

Figure 1. North Aleutian Basin proposed oil and gas lease site (hatched) overlain with pelagic trawls, 1990-2007.

ties. The Council is responsible for adopting stock assessments and a share-based allocation program, while day-to-day management and framework management structures are adopted by the Board. Under the crab FMP, nine crab fisheries have operated under a quota program for both harvesters and processors since 2002. The proposed oil and gas lease sale in the North Aleutian Basin overlaps with prime locations of Bristol Bay red king crab harvests (Fig. 2). The North Aleutian Basin site also overlaps with fishing grounds that generated 2% of the total Alaska scallop catch. The Council has deferred management to the Board for certain nearshore rockfishes, lingcod, and all salmon species; however, a federal oversight/appeals process is included to assure compliance with federal requirements in the federal exclusive economic zone (EEZ).

Management measures adopted in each of these Bering Sea and Aleutian Islands fisheries have restricted fishery growth or allocated harvests, or provided for reductions in the number of operating vessels (collectively called fishery rationalization). Development of these programs, whether through the Council or State of Alaska process, was achieved through a deliberative and transparent process in which resource managers and industry participants weighed conservation,

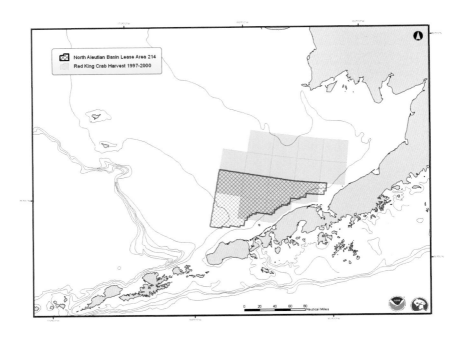

Figure 2. North Aleutian Basin proposed oil and gas lease site (hatched) overlain with Bristol Bay red king crab harvest, 1997-2000 (blue).

safety, economic efficiency, and distributional considerations. These programs take years to develop with intensive analysis and stakeholder input. While expected outcomes include improved conservation, safety, and economic returns to participants who remain in the fishery, costs are considerable. Some historic participants are excluded from the fishery, opportunities for new entrants are lessened, monitoring measures are heightened, and participants must strictly adhere to scientific-based harvest level specifications where the long-term stock health outweighs immediate economic gain. Managers and participants have weighed the long-term benefits that could be achieved through the implementation of the management programs in fisheries in or adjacent to the North Aleutian Basin against the immediate costs incurred for rationalizing these fisheries. These decisions were made in the absence of risks associated with oil and gas activity.

Fundamental to the Council's success in conserving these abundant and valuable marine resources is a strict reliance on annual catch quotas (total allowable catch) for all managed groundfish species and guideline harvest levels for crab and scallops. State and federal agencies expend millions of dollars to assess stocks and determine appropriate management. A large and highly complex public process involving industry participants, environmentalists, and agency researchers and managers from Alaska, Oregon, and Washington supports this fishery management process. The Council relies on sound science to establish the upper limits for those quotas, as well as for review of all other proposed management measures. Stock assessments are prepared annually by the Alaska Fisheries Science Center for groundfish and Alaska Department of Fish and Game for crabs and scallops; these assessments are reviewed by the Council's Plan Teams and Scientific and Statistical Committee (SSC), composed of agency and university scientists with expertise in stock assessment, fish population dynamics, socioeconomics, marine mammals, seabirds, and ecological/ecosystem function. The SSC provides the final recommendations on overfishing levels and allowable biological catch levels (ABCs) for each managed stock. The Council then sets the quotas at or below the ABC levels. The Council has a long-standing cap of 2 million metric tons of groundfish in the BSAI to accommodate ecosystem considerations, regardless of biomass increases that otherwise could allow the Council to increase quotas above the cap. The Board also has a science-based approach to set guideline harvest levels for state-managed fisheries and escapement goals within salmon fisheries. The Board manages harvest of sport, personal use/subsistence, and commercial fisheries resources.

Several Marine Protected Areas have been established by the Council in the region primarily to conserve crab and benthic habitat (Fig. 3). The Nearshore Bristol Bay Closure (19,000 nm^2) was established primarily for the conservation of juvenile red king crab habitat and is closed to all trawling. The Red King Crab Savings Area closed 4,000 nm^2 to bottom trawl and dredge gear primarily for the protection of red king crab adult habitat. Area 516, also in the Bristol Bay region, closed 4,000 nm^2 to bottom trawling seasonally for the protection of red king crab when molting. Protection measures were put in place for juvenile blue king crab habitat through a closure to all trawling in the Pribilof Islands Habitat Conservation Area, 7,000 nm^2. The Council closed 277,000 nm^2 to bottom trawl gear in the Aleutian Islands, while only 12,000 nm^2 remained open to bottom trawls. Additionally, farther north within an area affected by ocean currents, an area of 264,000 nm^2 was closed to bottom trawling to accommodate Bering Sea conservation concerns. These measures were adopted to ensure lasting protection of the habitats that support the continued production of healthy fishery resources. The Aleutian Islands area also has widespread closure areas to protect the endangered Steller sea lion. Any negative impacts to benthic habitat or Steller sea lion recovery resulting from new oil and gas activity in the North Aleutian Basin would potentially undermine the benefits gained by the Council's conservation efforts.

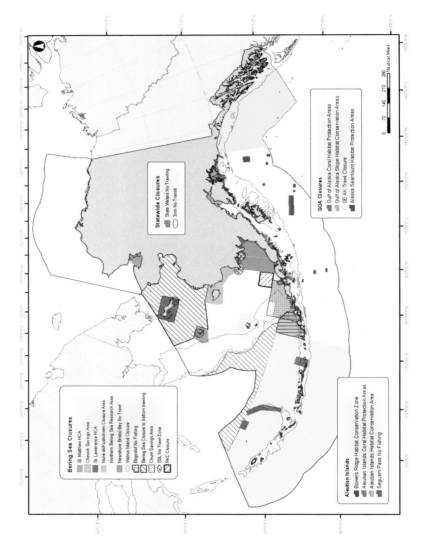

Figure 3. Conservation closures.

In light of its precautionary management measures to protect marine resources and habitat in the BSAI, the Council and the State of Alaska would be concerned about oil and gas exploration and development that may impact valuable commercial fisheries. These include (1) user conflicts—mooring cables, oil/gas supply lines, and vessels for petroleum extraction; (2) operational noise or spill impacts to endangered marine mammals and other marine species; and (3) additional usage provides additional opportunity for importing invasive species, groundings, and oiled habitat.

Thanks are extended to John Olson (National Marine Fisheries Service) and Cathy Coon (North Pacific Fishery Management Council) who prepared the figures for this report.

Questions and answers

Q: Has there been any habitat change because of these last several years of warmer temperatures and is there any buildup of habitat change going farther and farther north?

EARL KRYGIER: Habitat does not change quickly. Most of the bottom habitat includes different kinds of grasses, plants, and corals. Those areas are more stable and take longer to change. The shallow water corals in the tropics are more likely to be faced with acidification issues. We have seen different types of organisms pop up in water columns. The last few years have seen seasonal migrations moving farther north by about 20 miles a year.

Q: Have you noticed any impacts of 3-D seismic activity on the different fisheries?

EARL KRYGIER: There has been concern over the impacts of seismic on marine mammals. I don't know of any impacts on actual fisheries.

Q: You talked about 277,000 square nautical miles of closed areas for habitat protection. How much of that is in the Bowers Ridge area north of the Aleutians and had anyone fished out there prior to the closure?

EARL KRYGIER: We had some fishing. I think the point of the closure of that whole area was precautionary. Some of the largest stocks of fish that are harvested out from this area west are Atka mackerel and rockfish. We were being precautionary in trying to freeze the footprint of where most of the fishing occurred, in areas that were not coral or rock. People were trying to fish in areas between the rocks and on the sandy bottoms.

I can tell you from experience that gear modifications enable people to fish areas where they didn't before. I think it's important to understand that there are lots of different species in deeper water that people have not fished yet. By closing those areas ahead of time, we're encouraging those fisheries not to occur.

Q: I'm from Shell. Would you describe the stocks in general as being overfished, under-fished, or sustainably fished? Is there any particular species that are under pressure at this location?

EARL KRYGIER: Fisheries are managed for sustainability. The big fisheries in this area are the pollock, cod, flatfish, and rockfish. In the pollock fishery, we had a harvest of around 1.4 million metric tons a couple of years ago. This year we're right at about a million metric tons on harvest. The arrowtooth is one of the large growing stocks. The largest one, I believe, is the yellowfin sole. There is a precautionary cap on how much can be harvested. Precautionary harvest levels are set based on abundance. The National Marine Fisheries Service conducts annual surveys every summer to assess how healthy the stocks are. Then exploitation rates are set based not on the total population, but on the population of the spawning adults. The remainder of the population is left out of the equation as part of a safety valve. The spawning biomass is used to determine an acceptable biological harvest rate for each species based on the size of the spawning adult population. The number is very close to 3 million metric tons of harvest this year. But there is an artificial cap set at 2 million metric tons. So that cap leaves a very large, almost a million metric tons, of available harvest for the rest of the ecosystem.

Blue king crab stocks are quite depressed, but we've done some restricted fishing in the Pribilof Islands, so there won't be any impact either from the directed fishery or the groundfish fishery. Red king crab stocks are still down, but it looks like they're starting to build. The Bristol Bay red king crab stock is around 13 to 20 million harvested over the last 20 years. That's a pretty healthy fishery because it has been protected from most fishery impacts that could occur. We're very cautious on the types of gear we use, and we require escape panels in pot gear to provide an escape mechanism for pots that become lost. The snow crab fishery numbers have been very high and very low. They've been as high as 300 million and as low as eight million. The Tanner crab fishery has been depressed. I don't know if it was overfished because we had conservative management. We've been attempting to rebuild it because it's a very valuable fishery. The brown crab fisheries have been ongoing, producing around 6 billion pounds of crab.

North Aleutian Basin Energy-Fisheries Decisions: Could Structured Decision-Making Help?

Graham Long, Partner
*Compass Resource Management Ltd., Vancouver,
British Columbia, Canada*

Introduction

The question of the future role of energy exploitation in the North Aleutian Basin is a complex and important one. All choices, from "not on your life" to "full steam ahead" and variations in between, have different implications (real and perceived) for different people. What these implications might be, at the moment, are being left to the imaginations and experiences of each individual. Perspectives on "what to do" are being based on gut-level reactions to a vaguely defined question and the poorly understood implications of poorly defined alternatives.

This messiness is not inevitable. It just requires a commitment to a more organized approach to openly exploring the issue.

Structured decision-making (sometimes referred to as decision analysis) is an approach to organizing complicated decisions. It's based on the simple and commonsense idea that there are pros and cons (trade-offs) associated with any course of action, and that only by understanding the precise pros and cons of several alternative approaches can we, collectively, even begin to discuss which is the best (or "least worst") option for us all.

Let's suppose I asked you: which fruit should I buy from the store—apples or oranges? Unless you have a strong dislike for one or the other, your answer should probably be: "it depends." It depends on a number of factors that we all use to pick between options. In this case, the factors might include price, freshness, condition (whether or not they've been bruised) and, if we're really diligent, we might get to taste a sample of each. Only once we've compared the performance of the store's specific apples and the store's specific oranges can we decide between them.

The question of whether "apples" as such are better than "oranges" as such is pretty meaningless.

If we were buying large amounts of apples or oranges on behalf of other people, we might think of sketching out a little table to summarize the differences, like the one below:

	The store's apples	The store's oranges
Price ($/lb)	$ 1.20	$1.80
Freshness	Fresh in today	Look like they've been sitting around a while...
Condition	A bit bruised but generally OK	Fine
Taste	Tastes like a raw potato	Full of flavor

This is helpful in a number of ways. First, it helps communicate to others what the decision is all about. Second, it exposes what I think are the trade-offs between them in one table that we can think about all at once with no problem. Should we go with the fresh, less expensive (per lb) apples that taste like potatoes, or the older, more expensive but great tasting oranges? This is a question anyone can answer. Personally I'd go for the oranges. I don't mind the difference in price and I hate apples that taste like raw potatoes. But I'd be able to understand why you might disagree (maybe the per-lb price difference is more important to you, and that the potato-ness won't be such a problem if you intend to cover them with sugar and make a pie out of them). But that's fine— the point is we're agreeing on what the differences are between these particular apples and these particular oranges. What we disagree about is what's important to us about these differences. Half of the problem in complex decisions is actually understanding what the alternatives are, and ensuring that we're talking about the same things.

Of course, not many of us would sketch out a table like this for every little choice we have to make. But some decisions are just too important and too complicated not to be more organized. The future of oil exploitation in the North Aleutian Basin, I'd suggest, is a good example.

Steps in the decision structuring process

Structured decision-making typically encourages us to take the following steps. We can move up and down between these steps as we add more detail and make corrections, but generally we move through them in order.

1. Define the decision

2. Set objectives and evaluation criteria

3. Create alternatives

4. Assess consequences

5. Analyze trade-offs and decide

1. Define the decision

In the fruit example, I defined the decision as a choice between two types of fruit from a given store. I made up these constraints, of course, and you'd probably want to challenge them: why not buy some apples and some oranges? Why not take a look at what they have at the next store? Why not skip the fruit altogether and buy a candy bar? Maybe come back next Tuesday? All of these are fair points—you simply need to be clear how you want to put the question.

In the case of the North Aleutian Basin, defining the problem is harder. Is the question the one I introduced at the top: "What is the future role of energy exploitation in the North Aleutian Basin?" Or is it, "What might our communities look like in 20 years?" Or is it, "What levels of oil exploitation might we consider OK in which areas?" Or is it, "How can the oil and fisheries industries best serve the needs of local communities?" Or is it, "Should we allow oil exploration, yes or no?" There are many more ways of framing the problem—you need to get together and pick one that you can all live with.

2. Set objectives and evaluation criteria

In the fruit example, I guessed that you might be interested in cost, freshness, and so on.

In the case of the North Aleutian Basin, there are clearly more objectives. These probably include such things as environmental impacts (e.g., impacts on endangered species, etc.), local economic impacts (e.g., revenues to communities, jobs, etc.), revenues to industry (e.g., oil company revenues, fishery industry revenues, etc.), impacts on local ways of life (i.e., how might people's lives will be changed as a result of doing one thing rather than another?), and so on. Again, only by sitting down together can we figure out what all the issues are.

3. Create alternatives

In the fruit example, I gave you the option of apples versus oranges.

In the case of the North Aleutian Basin, the range of alternatives available depends on how you define the question. You might, for example, decide to explore several scenarios of oil exploitation (different sizes and scales, different technologies, different locations) in order to get some idea of what might happen. In this case, you can't know in advance which particular option will happen (since it's dependent on the outcome of test drilling), but it could be possible to explore a number of "what if" situations.

4. Assess consequences

In the fruit example, I guessed at the consequences of buying apples versus oranges. Some of the consequences are well known (e.g., the price per lb). Other consequences might not be as well known (e.g., eating a sample of one apple does not necessarily mean that when I get home all the apples will taste like a raw potato).

In the case of the North Aleutian Basin, the uncertainties surrounding the impacts are greater. We don't know for sure how a development of such-and-such a size in such-and-such a location might affect salmon returns, for example. We don't know for sure, but we know something. There might be computer models that can help. Or maybe we could ask a panel of experts for their opinion on the probability that certain outcomes would happen under specific circumstances (there are well established best practices in the academic literature for doing this). Think this is too tricky? Well, first of all, we are doing this anyway when we make a judgment as to which alternative is best—isn't it better to be explicit and open about it? Isn't it better to get the best available information? Also, we're not asking experts for the correct answer—we're asking for a description of the range of uncertainty they would have under very well described scenarios (e.g., "how much more likely are problems for salmon under alternative A than alternative B?")

5. Assess trade-offs and decide

In the fruit example, I looked at the whole table and decided I preferred the oranges. I was able to assess the trade-offs between price, freshness, and the other issues, to make a choice, and to describe why I made the choice by referring to the rows in the table.

In the case of the North Aleutian Basin, assessing the consequences of alternatives would be more complex, because there would be more alternatives and more rows to balance across them. But the same principle applies. There are many tools and techniques we have to help explore and understand the consequences of complex options. But the table of consequences is simply that: a table of consequences. The decision about "what to do" should be the result of discussion about that table, and what's important about it to different people. Through discussion, it might be possible to agree never to allow certain scenarios, or to agree to cautiously proceed with some others.

Conclusion

For the North Aleutian Basin fisheries, energy discussions now under way are at once extremely important and complex. They are easily far too complex for even the most highly informed and experienced individual to keep all factors in mind at once. Perhaps more importantly, most people have no real idea how various forms of oil exploitation scenarios might affect a whole host of issues that they consider important. Until reasonable alternative courses of action are explored (or, initially at least, different possible external outcomes resulting from exploration and subsequent exploitation), meaningful discussion about "what to do" will be challenging indeed, and no one could be blamed for resorting to more emotional, gut-level responses. A structured approach to organizing and discussing this problem along the lines suggested here would not be easy, but could offer a helpful approach to truly engaging people in genuine discussion about the choices that will shape their future for generations to come.

Questions and answers

Q: I think the most important issue is defining the problem.

GRAHAM LONG: I couldn't agree more. I would encourage you to sit down and ask yourself some questions. What are we doing? Is it possible to explore for oil without harming fisheries? What's the best way of exploring for oil without harming fisheries? You have to come up with your own list of questions and explore them.

Q: How does your process involve Native groups?

GRAHAM LONG: Every decision is different, and the role of every party depends on their regulatory and jurisdictional interest. In a fisheries resource case in Canada, First Nations were invited early on but chose not to attend, and I don't blame them. There was only a month before a decision was going to be made. They were involved informally toward the end, but in the planning process they were involved right from the beginning.

Q: I'm from Canada and I understand the whole fisheries situation. In Canada we have many forums where we go through exercises like this, but at the end of the day, a political decision is made. This takes away from the whole process and people become very skeptical.

GRAHAM LONG: I agree. Political issues usually push a minister's hand to do something other than what the process has come up with. It's important at the beginning to clarify the roles and responsibilities of what this decision is all about. It's actually better if there is a separate decision maker as in this situation where the governor will make a final call.

If a group cannot reach a final agreement, the decision maker is willing to step in and make the call. It would be difficult, though, if a group reached an agreement and the minister overturned it for reasons that were not clear.

Q: Should risk assessment in the decision-making process be done by an independent in every case?

GRAHAM LONG: I'm not sure that I'm qualified to answer that question. I see risk assessment as being one ingredient in understanding the matrix. I guess it is a question of trust. Do you trust the people to define the scope of the question, to do the field tests with integrity, and to report their findings accurately? I think it is context-dependent.

Panel

Meeting the Environmental Challenge in the North Aleutian Basin

World Wildlife Fund on Bristol Bay Oil and Gas Development

Bubba Cook, Senior Fisheries Officer
World Wildlife Fund, Anchorage, Alaska

Alaska's Bristol Bay and the southeastern Bering Sea encompass one of the most productive marine ecosystems in the world. These subarctic waters support important commercial fisheries, representing more than 40% of the nation's annual seafood catch. The area targeted for oil and gas leasing, known as the North Aleutian Basin, overlaps with important habitat and fishing grounds for pollock, cod, red king crab, halibut, and salmon fisheries which generate more than $2 billion annually. These fisheries support fishermen and fishing families throughout Alaska and the Pacific Northwest, as well as numerous vibrant coastal communities in the Bristol Bay region.

Bristol Bay sockeye salmon runs, the largest on earth, are the lifeblood of many remote, Native villages in southwestern Alaska. Subsistence and commercial harvests of salmon resources are the economic mainstay of these culturally unique communities.

The region's coastal wetlands, lagoons, and sheltered bays serve as migratory hubs, staging areas, and wintering grounds for millions of waterfowl and shorebirds. The southeastern Bering Sea is also home to a number of marine mammal species—many of which are threatened or endangered—including sea otters, Steller sea lions, fur seals, humpback whales, and the North Pacific right whale. As a testament to the region's ecological importance, five National Wildlife Refuges and eight Alaska state protected areas have been established here.

For these and many other reasons, the National Marine Fisheries Service (NMFS) of the National Oceanic and Atmospheric Administration concluded in comments to the Minerals Management Service (MMS) that "the proposed leasing schedule is unrealistically ambitious and would not allow for necessary environmental research to support NEPA analysis and MMS's leasing process." NMFS recommended the "deletion of these areas and initiations of a comprehensive research program to support future plans subsequent to the 2007-2012 plan." Additionally, the North Aleutian Basin Information Status and Research Planning meeting in December 2006, convened by the MMS, identified that significant data gaps exist with respect to oil and gas development impacts on fisheries. The meeting identified critical needs for baseline information on benthic communities, intertidal communities specific to Bristol Bay, and fish species distribution, abundance, and life history data.

At the same time, the safety of oil and gas operations has failed to significantly improve since a moratorium on OCS (outer continental shelf) development was put in place almost 20 years ago. Between 1985 and 1999, there were 19,506 spills between 0 and 42 gallons (1 bbl) from OCS platforms and pipelines around the nation. Chronic oil pollution is a serious threat to many aquatic life forms. Oil can be toxic to fish, crabs, shellfish, and other invertebrates at very small quantities and chronic exposure can cause a range of lethal and sublethal effects on these organisms such as mutations and reduced reproductive capacity. New science continues to show the adverse effects of hydrocarbon contamination on marine organisms.

Additionally, spills associated with oil and gas pipeline operations have only improved marginally during the same period. OCS pipeline spill occurrence rates for spills greater than or equal to 1,000 bbl have remained essentially unchanged since 1980. Published reports indicate there have been eight large spills from OCS pipelines between 1985 and 1999, with an average spill size of 6,700 bbl (281,400 gallons). The risk associated with pipelines is further highlighted by BP's pipeline spill on March 2, 2006, which resulted in 267,000 gallons of oil spilling onto the arctic tundra.

In an area as harsh and unforgiving as the Bering Sea, the risk becomes even more significant. As popularized in the TV series *Deadliest Catch*, the Bering Sea is home to some of the most violent storm and ice conditions in the world with wind gusts over 100 miles per hour and wave heights approaching 50 feet. These extreme conditions are comparable to Hurricane Katrina in 2005, which had wind speeds greater than 120 miles per hour and a maximum-recorded wave height of 55.5 feet—a record matched only in the Aleutian Islands in January 1991. In May 2006, MMS published its offshore damage assessment from Hurricane Katrina, which indicated that 113 platforms were totally destroyed and 457 pipelines were damaged with 101 of pipelines 10 inches or larger diameter. At least 741,000 gallons were spilled from 124 reported sources in the months following Hurricane Katrina.

WWF believes the value of safeguarding the Bering Sea's renewable fish and wildlife resources far outweighs the low potential of oil and gas and the associated risks of offshore development activities. Indeed, the risks of oil and gas development remain virtually unchanged since the moratorium on oil and gas development in Bristol Bay was established and supported by many Alaskans in the 1990s. The threats, spills, infrastructure effects, adverse marketing effects, and grounds preemption, remain no less of a concern than they were 20 years ago. The proposed benefits remain limited in time, scope, and magnitude in comparison to the existing values of the Bering Sea. Additionally, significant gaps in oil spill response and shipping safety in the region further contribute to this elevated risk. Given the relatively small amounts of finite oil and gas resources located in the proposed lease sale area and the risk it poses to the prolific and sustainable fisheries resources, oil and gas development in the proposed lease sale area is simply not justified. More important, these risks will be predominantly borne by fishermen and communities, while any potential benefit goes to a relative few in the oil and gas industry.

In summary, the commercial and intrinsic value of the region's marine life is too great to put at risk for the small amount of estimated recoverable oil reserves in the North Aleutian Basin. We should not allow the cultural, ecological, and economic significance of the renewable fisheries resources to be jeopardized by a short-term, finite development project. Moreover, this forum has failed to ask the right question, which is not how oil and gas development in Bristol Bay will proceed safely, but whether it should be allowed in Bristol Bay in the first place. For these reasons, WWF supports the preservation and promotion of the fisheries, development of alternative energy, and support of a renewable and sustainable economic base in the region rather than finite oil and gas development in Bristol Bay.

Bristol Bay and Southeast Bering Sea Fisheries: Renewable Riches Worth Protecting

Kelly Harrell, Friends of Bristol Bay Coordinator
Alaska Marine Conservation Council, Anchorage, Alaska

After 17 years of federal protection, Alaska's fish-rich Bristol Bay and southeastern Bering Sea are once again being targeted for offshore oil and gas development. Best known for producing the world's largest wild salmon runs, Bristol Bay and the southeastern Bering Sea represent one of the most productive marine ecosystems on earth. The Bering Sea accounts for more than 50% of U.S. fish and shellfish landings and is often referred to as the nation's "fish basket."[1] The area proposed for oil and gas leasing falls within the heart of waters teeming with renewable, living marine riches that support important fisheries and communities across Alaska that depend on them.

Fisheries jeopardized

Bristol Bay and southeastern Bering Sea commercial fisheries that could be jeopardized by offshore oil and gas activities are extremely important economically, with a combined total annual value of more than $2 billion.[2] Commercial fishing is the economic mainstay of southwest Alaska's communities and provides the primary source of income and jobs for the region's residents. Subsistence harvest of salmon and other fish continues to supply a vital source of traditional food for Alaska Natives and remains integral to Native cultures throughout western Alaska. Offshore oil and gas activities present a wide spectrum of potential impacts to these economically, ecologically, and culturally important fisheries resources of the Bristol Bay region.

---

[1] Arctic Research Consortium of the United States. 2004. Bering Sea ecosystem study (BEST) science plan. Fairbanks, Alaska.

[2] Alaska Marine Conservation Council. 2008. Economic value of Bristol Bay and southeastern Bering Sea fisheries. http://www.akmarine.org/our-work/protect-bristol-bay/commercial-fisheries-value-feb-08.

Seismic surveys

Marine seismic surveys are used to determine the location of oil and gas deposits beneath the seafloor. These surveys generate powerful, underwater noise that can kill adult fish, larvae, and fish eggs within close proximity of firing air guns.[3] Scientific studies have also shown that seismic air gun blasts can cause a variety of sublethal impacts to fish and their prey including physical damage to tissues and organs such as ears and swim bladders.[4] Studies conducted in the North Sea demonstrated that fish catch rates can be dramatically reduced (by more than 50%) for several days as a result of seismic surveys that cause fish to flee an area.[5] More research is needed to determine the potential effects of seismic activity on economically valuable populations of red king crab that carry out sensitive phases of their life cycle in the region.

Potential pollution

Additionally, offshore oil and gas operations produce a number of waste streams that can pollute the surrounding aquatic environment and alter living seafloor communities. The federal Minerals Management Service (MMS) has stated that in Bristol Bay, more than 10,440 tons of drill cuttings ". . . generated during exploratory drilling would be discharged directly at the drill sites and, thus, could adversely affect nearby water quality."[6] The permitted discharge of thousands of tons of drilling wastes into Bristol Bay is a major concern given that these waters provide vital fish habitat for a variety of commercial species that dwell on the seafloor, including crab and juvenile halibut. Drilling discharges can kill marine organisms by smothering and toxic exposure. Discharges can also cause sublethal effects to fish eggs, fry, and invertebrates in the mixing zone even at volumes permitted by the Environmental

---

[3] McCauley et al. 2000. Marine seismic surveys: A study of environmental implications. Australian Petroleum Production and Exploration Association Journal 2000:692-708. http://www.cwr.org.au/publications/appea2000.pdf.

[4] McCauley et al. 2002. High intensity anthropogenic sound damages fish ears. Journal of the Acoustical Society of America 113(1):638-642.

[5] Engas et al. 1993. Effects of seismic shooting on catch and catch-availability of cod and haddock. Fisken og Havet 9:99-117.

Lokkeborg and Soldal. 1993. The influence of seismic exploration with airgun on cod (*Gadus morhua*) behavior and catch rates. ICES Marine Science Symposium 196:62-67.

Skalski et al. 1992. Effects of sound from geophysical surveys device on catch-per-unit-effort in a hook-and-line fishery for rockfish (*Sebastes* spp.). Canadian Journal of Fisheries and Aquatic Sciences 49:1357-1365.

[6] U.S. Minerals Management Service (MMS). April 2007. Proposed Outer Continental Shelf Oil and Gas Leasing Program: 2007-2012. Final Environmental Impact Statement, pp. IV-115. http://www.mms.gov/5-year/2007-2012_FEIS.htm.

Protection Agency (EPA).[7] Studies in the Gulf of Mexico have shown that drilling discharges can cause long-term, negative biological and physical changes to seafloor habitats and can lead to the presence of contaminants in sediments and fish tissues, including heavy metals such as mercury.[8] Disposal of drill cuttings can alter habitat suitability for bottom-dwelling fish and shellfish, potentially causing disturbance and dislocation of groundfish and crab in the area.[9]

Infrastructure impact

The process of getting oil and gas to markets also greatly enlarges the footprint of offshore fossil fuel development with a significant portion of activities occurring in highly sensitive and biologically important coastal areas. The envisioned transportation route for mobilizing Bristol Bay's oil and gas calls for pipelines through coastal habitats within Herendeen Bay and the Port Moller State Critical Habitat Area. The pipelines would make landfall and run onshore across the Alaska Peninsula Wildlife Refuge. Processing facilities, including a potential liquefied natural gas (LNG) plant, would be located on the southern side of the Alaska Peninsula and tankers would travel through the Gulf of Alaska near Kodiak Island to carry the oil and/or gas to markets. Pipeline and other infrastructure construction in these rich coastal areas would cause habitat degradation and loss, including wetlands and eelgrass beds, which serve as important fish habitat. Increased turbidity, increased siltation, and increased contaminant loads in salmon streams along the transportation route could result in decreased salmon production in the area.[10] Additionally, placement of pipelines, platforms, and wells would disturb and degrade benthic habitat within important juvenile and nursery grounds for halibut and red king crab. The presence of infrastructure could also cause displacement from important fishing grounds leading to a reduction in fishing area, and may result in lost or damaged gear that could reduce fishing time and cause loss of income.[11]

---

[7] MMS. April 2007, pp. IV-182.

[8] Paul Montagna. GOOMEX: Experimental design and what the data mean. Minerals Management Service Web site. http://www.mms.gov/eppd/scicom/sc_mercury/goomex_presentation.htm.

Peterson et al. 1996. Ecological consequences of environmental perturbations associated with offshore hydrocarbon production: A perspective on long-term exposures in the Gulf of Mexico. Canadian Journal of Fisheries and Aquatic Sciences 53:2367-2654.

[9] MMS. April 2007, pp. IV-175 and IV-182.

[10] MMS. April 2007, pp. IV-B-26.

[11] MMS. April 2007, pp. IV 256-259.

Spill risk

Oil spills, however, have the potential to cause the most severe impacts in Bristol Bay and the southeastern Bering Sea. While the environmental track record of offshore oil and gas operations has improved over past years, oil spills remain the rule rather than the exception when the overall life span of an oil and gas operation is considered. The federal government itself has predicted at least one large spill and numerous smaller spills will occur if oil and gas development takes place in Bristol Bay.[12] The oil spill risk is exacerbated by the high frequency of volcanic and earthquake activity in the region as well as by the Bering Sea's infamous storms that can produce hurricane-strength winds. Rough weather and the presence of sea ice, which can extend into the lease sale area in heavy ice years, would severely hinder spill cleanup efforts during a large portion of the year. The effects of an oil spill within a region so biologically rich and so heavily dependent on living marine resources would be tremendous and long lasting. Oil spills could lead to fisheries closures and cause devastating economic loss. Potential long-term marketing effects could result from even the mere perception that seafood products were tainted. Damage to subsistence resources and the opportunity to carry out traditional practices would have profound consequences for indigenous peoples of the region.

Essential fish habitat

A number of commercially important species utilize the region's shallow continental shelf during critical life activities, thereby enhancing the risk that long-term, population-level consequences could result from oil and gas activities. Bristol Bay salmon have juvenile migratory routes, key juvenile growth and feeding areas, as well as adult migratory routes that directly overlap and occur around the proposed lease sale area. Nursery grounds that support the entire North Pacific halibut population fall directly within the lease sale area.[13] Essential fish habitat for all life stages of Bristol Bay red king crab overlap the lease sale area and nearly 100% of the red king crab harvest comes from within the sale area.[14] Essential fish habitat for all life stages of pollock—the largest single-species fishery in the world—occurs within and surrounding

---

[12] MMS. April 2007, pp. IV-115.

[13] International Pacific Halibut Commission. 1998. The Pacific halibut: Biology, fishery, and management. Technical Report no. 40.

[14] National Marine Fisheries Service. April 2005. Final Environmental Impact Statement for Essential Fish Habitat Identification and Conservation in Alaska, Appendix D. http://www.fakr.noaa.gov/habitat/seis/final/Volume_II/Appendix_D.pdf.

Evans, D. Nov. 28-Dec. 1, 2006. North Pacific Fishery Management Council. Federal fisheries of the North Aleutian Basin. PowerPoint presented at the North Aleutian Basin Information Status and Research Planning Meeting, Anchorage, Alaska.

the area proposed for leasing.[15] Pacific cod and various flatfish species including yellowfin sole, flathead sole, and rock sole also have essential fish habitat within the waters slated for drilling.

Economics

The potential benefits of offshore oil and gas development pale in comparison to the ecological, economic, and cultural value of the renewable fisheries resources of Bristol Bay and the southeast Bering Sea. Offshore oil and gas development in Bristol Bay's waters would do little to reduce our nation's dependence on foreign energy and would provide limited local, regional, and statewide benefits. While certain negative effects might be mitigated, the risk of a major accident that could have long-term, devastating impacts on the region's renewable fisheries resources can never be wholly eliminated. From a variety of vantage points—local, regional, and national, as well as economic, social, and ecological—the risk is simply not worth taking. Renewable energy resources exist in the Bristol Bay region that could provide long-term, lower-cost energy to residents while creating additional economic opportunities that are consistent with a fisheries-based economy. The best fisheries, economic, and energy policy requires protecting the renewable riches of Bristol Bay and the southeastern Bering Sea from offshore oil and gas development.

About the Alaska Marine Conservation Council

The Alaska Marine Conservation Council is a community-based organization dedicated to protecting the long-term health of Alaska's marine ecosystems and sustaining the working waterfronts of our coastal communities. Our board and members include commercial and sport fishermen, subsistence harvesters, small business owners, marine scientists, and coastal residents throughout Alaska. Our way of life, livelihoods, and economies depend upon healthy marine ecosystems.

---

[15] NMFS. April 2005.

Meeting the Environmental Challenge in the North Aleutian Basin

Jon Kurland, Assistant Regional Administrator for Habitat Conservation
NOAA National Marine Fisheries Service, Juneau, Alaska

The prospect of energy development in the North Aleutian Basin is a matter of great interest to those concerned with the protection and sustainable management of the region's natural resources. The National Oceanic and Atmospheric Administration's National Marine Fisheries Service (NOAA Fisheries) is responsible for stewardship of living marine resources through science-based conservation and management and the promotion of healthy ecosystems. We have three principal natural resource programs: Sustainable Fisheries, which implements fishery management programs for groundfish, crabs, and scallops; Protected Resources, which is responsible for the protection and recovery of marine mammals and endangered species; and Habitat Conservation, which provides technical assistance and funding to protect and restore the habitats that support sustainable fisheries and marine mammals.

The importance of Alaska's marine resources is well known. Alaska waters provide half of all U.S. seafood. The seafood industry is the largest private sector employer in Alaska. Subsistence fisheries and marine mammal harvests are very important for Alaskans. Alaska has significant ocean-dependent coastal communities, and Alaska fishing ports consistently rank among the top in the United States in landings and value. As Congress recognized in its statement of findings for the Magnuson-Stevens Fishery Conservation and Management Act, "One of the greatest long-term threats to the viability of commercial and recreational fisheries is the continuing loss of marine, estuarine, and other aquatic habitats." If we want to protect the bounty that derives from the eastern Bering Sea, we need to take good care of the habitat.

The concern about energy development in the North Aleutian Basin is clear: potential adverse effects on fish stocks, marine mammals, human users, and other components of the ecosystem. As the Minerals Management Service noted in its 2008 Alaska Annual Studies Plan, "It would be difficult to identify an area in the Bering Sea, or possibly anywhere in the world that has greater fisheries, protected species, or human use issues than this proposed sale area."

Other speakers at this workshop are describing the fisheries prosecuted in Bristol Bay, the Aleutian Islands, and the eastern Bering Sea as well as the marine mammals and the importance of all these resources for local communities, so I'll only mention a couple of examples here. First is the area identified as critical habitat for the highly endangered North Pacific right whale. The size of this population is unknown but certainly less than 100 individuals, and probably much less. Observations by NOAA Fisheries' National Marine Mammal Laboratory over the past few decades have consistently highlighted use of the southeastern Bering Sea as right whale feeding habitat. The North Aleutian Basin is also identified as Essential Fish Habitat (EFH) for a wide array of commercially important species under the Magnuson-Stevens Fishery Conservation and Management Act. NOAA Fisheries and the North Pacific Fishery Management Council have identified EFH for 34 species in this area, including staples of tremendously valuable commercial fisheries: walleye pollock, Pacific cod, flatfishes, several species of rockfishes, red king crabs, and all five species of Pacific salmon.

What is NOAA's role in reviewing development proposals for the North Aleutian Basin? NOAA Fisheries will continue to assist regulatory agencies, industries, and other stakeholders in several ways. We will participate in the environmental impact analysis of any proposed actions that may adversely affect living marine resources and their habitats. We will consult with the federal action agencies under the Endangered Species Act and Magnuson-Stevens Act. We will recommend measures to avoid, minimize, or offset adverse effects. We will also provide technical assistance, share available data, and help identify data gaps.

The environmental review process for energy development in the North Aleutian Basin should include analysis of the kinds of information necessary to make fully informed decisions: (1) available data from fish surveys, ichthyoplankton surveys, and commercial fisheries; (2) seasonal abundance, distribution, and condition of fish and marine mammals (offshore and nearshore); (3) reasonably foreseeable consequences of development (including accidents) for all ecosystem components: marine mammals, fish, plankton, birds; (4) effects on EFH and listed species (endangered or threatened); and (5) impact assessment methodologies that have been vetted through an inclusive and transparent process.

Finally, it is important to view potential energy development in the North Aleutian Basin in the context of other human effects on the ecosystem. Arguably commercial fishing is the human activity that currently has the greatest direct influence on marine resources in this area. The North Pacific Fishery Management Council (NPFMC) and NOAA Fisheries have implemented a series of recent and historic habitat protection measures in and around the North Aleutian Basin. Most of Bristol Bay has been closed to trawling and dredging since 1997 to protect crab habitat, except for a small area left open seasonally for a yellowfin sole trawl fishery that has low crab bycatch. The area around the Pribilof Islands has been closed to trawling and dredging since 1995 to protect juvenile blue king crabs. In 2006 most of the Aleutian Islands management area was closed to bottom trawling and some portions were closed to all bottom contact fishing gear to protect sensitive habitat features. In 2007 the NPFMC recommended closing another 130,000 square nautical miles of the Bering Sea to bottom trawling to protect habitat, and NOAA Fisheries is now promulgating the regulations to implement this latest closure. And of course, for over three decades the NPFMC and NOAA Fisheries have consistently set conservative catch limits for all managed stocks in the Bering Sea to ensure that none of the stocks become overfished. We have taken big steps to be precautionary in managing the effects of fisheries on habitat and the ecosystem, and we want to ensure good management of the effects of other human activities too.

North Alaska Peninsula

Bob Murphy, Salmon and Herring Area
Management Biologist
Alaska Department of Fish and Game, Port Moller, Alaska

The North Alaska Peninsula stretches 350 miles across the north side of the Alaska Peninsula from Cape Sarichef on Unimak Island to Cape Menshikof, which is the eastern boundary of the Bristol Bay salmon management area. Large-scale salmon fisheries occur along the shores of the North Alaska Peninsula. In the North Alaska Peninsula salmon fisheries, five species of Pacific salmon are harvested with significant chinook, coho, and chum salmon fisheries occurring in some locations. Although the sockeye salmon harvest is considerably smaller than the neighboring Bristol Bay harvest, the North Alaska Peninsula sockeye salmon harvest is typically one of the largest of all management areas in the state. The 2007 North Alaska Peninsula sockeye salmon catch was the third largest on record at just over 3.4 million fish. The 1988-2007 average value for the salmon fishery was $13.3 million. The average 20-year total salmon harvest for the North Alaska Peninsula is 2.6 million fish. The bulk of the escapement is sockeye salmon and occurs throughout the North Alaska Peninsula with the majority of the escapement monitored at four major systems with salmon counting weirs. The most recent 20-year average escapement was approximately 1.8 million salmon in North Alaska Peninsula river systems, of which just over 1 million were sockeye salmon.

There are several communities located within the Alaska Peninsula management area, including Port Heiden, Port Moller (seasonally), Sand Point, Nelson Lagoon, King Cove, Cold Bay, and False Pass with a year-round population of over 2,000 people. The residents of these communities rely on the salmon, groundfish, and shellfish resources of the area for subsistence purposes and for the commercial fisheries that support the economy of their communities.

The North Alaska Peninsula peak sac roe herring harvest and bio-mass estimate occurred in 1992 when over 28,000 tons of herring were observed and the harvest was 4,000 tons. Due to poor herring market conditions over the past 15 years, minimal harvest has occurred on the North Alaska Peninsula. The first harvest was in 1982, and harvest peaked in 1992. Historically, the bulk of the herring sac roe harvest has occurred on the North Alaska Peninsula, specifically in the areas that encompass Port Moller and Herendeen bays, Cape Seniavin, and occasionally in Port Heiden.

Domestic crab fisheries in the Bering Sea began in the Bristol Bay area in the 1950s. Harvest and effort have fluctuated annually, but have been relatively stable in recent years. Current fleet size is approximately 80 vessels, down from over 300 in the early 1990s. The fisheries are prosecuted between mid-October and the end of May. Bering Sea crab fisheries provide important revenue for the cities of Unalaska, St. Paul, King Cove, Akutan, St. George, and Kodiak. A large percentage of the Bristol Bay red king crab and Tanner crab fisheries occurs within the proposed lease area.

The Bristol Bay red king crab stock abundance is at the highest levels seen since the early 1980s. The 1998-2007 average for the Bristol Bay red king crab harvest and fishery value is 13.8 million pounds and $62 million. The stock status of the Bering Sea Tanner crab stock is improving but is below the levels seen in the early 1990s. The Tanner crab fishery was closed from 1997 to 2004 and since reopening, the average harvest and fishery value is 0.8 million pounds and $1.9 million. Stock density for snow (opilio) crab is greatest northwest of the Pribilof Islands, but distribution extends as far east as about 162 degrees west longitude. The commercial fishery occurs exclusively west of 166 degrees west longitude. Bering Sea snow crab stock status is trending upward and has a 1998-2007 average harvest and fishery value of 68.8 million pounds and $66.4 million.

The North Alaska Peninsula is home to three state critical habitat areas located at Cinder River, Port Heiden, and Port Moller, and one state game refuge, located at Izembek Lagoon. All of these areas have significant populations of brown bears. Other terrestrial mammals are present in varying concentrations including wolves, moose, and caribou. Harbor seals haul out and pup on outer beaches and offshore islands, and whales feed in the rich waters. These areas are utilized by the endangered western population of Steller sea lions and the threatened southwest Alaska population of northern sea otters. Approximately 35 miles east of Port Moller lies Cape Seniavin, which is located about 15 miles east of the Proposed Final Program Area, and is a known walrus haul-out that is part of the Bristol Bay complex of walrus. All of the criti-cal habitat areas, with their vast expanse of tidelands and wetlands, are important to hundreds of thousands of ducks, geese, and shorebirds, on their way to northern nesting grounds in the spring, and in the fall on their return to southern wintering grounds. These areas also provide nesting habitat for many birds including tundra swans, arctic and Aleutian terns, and common eiders. Also, Pacific herring spawn and rear in these areas. Izembek State Game Refuge is a prime waterfowl hunting area and bird-watching destination. Izembek Lagoon supports one of the largest eelgrass beds in the world and is a major migratory staging area for millions of waterfowl and shorebirds including most of the world's population of Pacific black brant, emperor goose, and the threatened Steller's eider, earning worldwide recognition as a "wetland of international importance." And of course, the rivers flowing into these critical habitat areas support all five species of Pacific salmon, important to subsistence users, sport anglers, and commercial fishers.

Citizens Promoting Environmentally Safe Operation of the Oil Industry in the North Aleutian Basin

John Devens, Executive Director
Prince William Sound Regional Citizens'
Advisory Council, Valdez, Alaska

An underlying principle of the Prince William Sound Regional Citizens' Advisory Council is that the citizens who have the most to lose in the event of an industrial accident should have a say in the prevention and response programs that are put in place. It is a true but unfortunate fact that in most cases little or nothing is done to involve local citizens until after a disaster occurs.

In the time I have I will describe some of the citizen organizations that have formed to help protect the environment in all its dimensions— natural, social, and economic—because all of those aspects suffer when oil is spilled.

Sullom Voe Association

In chronological order, we begin with the Sullom Voe Association (SVA) in the Shetland Islands of Scotland. The SVA was created in 1975 as an agreement between Shetland's local government or Council and more than 30 oil companies, with BP as the operating company.

SVA was established as a nonprofit corporation, to supervise the construction and operation of the Sullom Voe Terminal. All decisions are by consensus and industry pays all costs. The SVA appoints expert advisory groups including local special interest groups such as fishermen. The Council used eminent domain to acquire land that was leased back to industry—disagreement over rent lasted 15 years. The Council built and owned four tanker-loading jetties to be paid for by industry; repayments were the other major financial dispute.

The Council holds a 51% share in the tug company, which had exclusive rights until 2000. The Council took a share in a joint venture to run one of the construction companies. In addition to property tax, industry paid millions in "disturbance money" for the additional cost of providing infrastructure for industry during the construction boom. Industry paid between 1.6 and 3.2 cents US on every metric ton of oil shipped.

The Council established the Harbor Reserve Fund worth around $128 million US, and the Shetland Islands Council Charitable Trust worth around $350 million. They use oil money "for the benefit of the inhabitants of the Shetland Islands," including projects in social welfare, leisure, recreation, environmental education, and economic development.

Vigipol

Vigipol, formally the Syndicate Mixte, was created following the *Amoco Cadiz* spill in France in 1980. The board is made up of elected officials from the area affected by the *Amoco Cadiz* spill. Funding comes from part of the oil spill settlement. Vigipol has done a very good job of preventing complacency. In 1989 they sent a delegation to Alaska to provide assistance and advice.

Cook Inlet RCAC

The Cook Inlet RCAC was created by the Oil Pollution Act of 1990 (OPA 90). The Cook Inlet RCAC is similar to the Prince William Sound RCAC, but lacks the secure funding their sister organization enjoys. Cook Inlet RCAC's funding comes through negotiations with the oil industry and some funding from local municipalities.

Prince William Sound RCAC

The Prince William Sound RCAC was created in 1990 following the *Exxon Valdez* oil spill, and is mandated by OPA 90 and our contract with Alyeska Pipeline Service Company. The Prince William Sound RCAC has 19 board members broadly representative of municipalities, fishing, tourism, Native groups, and environmental groups in the 1989 oiled region. Our 2008 budget is approximately $3.8 million.

The oil industry has rightly received much public credit for the extensive prevention and response improvements made in Prince William Sound since 1989. What's less well known is that citizens were calling for improvements like these long before 1989. In fact, the calls began even before the first barrel of Prudhoe crude started down the trans-Alaska pipeline to Valdez in June 1977. Between the Prudhoe Bay oil strike in 1968 and the 1989 oil spill 21 years later, citizens called for, among other things, double-hull tankers, escort tugs, and comprehensive preparations for cleaning up an oil spill.

In 1986 the city of Valdez attempted to take matters into its own hands by imposing a special tax on oil-industry property, with the proceeds to be used for building and equipping an oil-spill response facility. The idea died because of a lawsuit by the State of Alaska, which argued successfully that Valdez lacked authority to levy the tax. Those calls, like the demands for better tankers and escort tugs, went unheeded until the 1989 oil spill made it clear the old way wasn't working.

In February 1990, Alyeska signed a contract with the Prince William Sound RCAC laying out its oversight powers and guaranteeing its funding. Today, Alyeska provides about $3.2 million annually, some 95% of total RCAC funding. The contract also guarantees the independence of Prince William Sound RCAC, which it referred to as the "Committee." In August 1990, Prince William Sound RCAC acquired federal authority when President George H.W. Bush signed into law the Oil Pollution Act of 1990.

Pipeline Safety Trust

The Pipeline Safety Trust (PST) was created in October 2003. It is funded by earnings from a $4 million criminal fine resulting from the June 10, 1999 Bellingham, Washington pipeline tragedy, in which three young people were killed. The PST has ten board members and three staff. It is totally independent of government and industry pressure. Its mission statement is "The PST promotes fuel transportation safety through education and advocacy, by increasing access to information, and by building partnerships with residents, safety advocates, government, and industry, that result in safer communities and a healthier environment."

Washington State Oil Spill Advisory Council

The Washington State Oil Spill Advisory Council was created in August 2005, by action of the Washington State Legislature. It reports to the Governor, and has a 13-member board consisting of a mixture of industry, government, fisheries, and environmental representatives. Currently there are three paid staff members. Their funding comes from state legislative appropriation.

Conclusion

Many of the achievements by the various citizen organizations have come despite initial opposition from the oil industry. As one can see from the above examples, a disaster is usually required before citizen oversight is established. If there is a lesson to be learned it is that negotiations should be done before development begins such that a strong, independent, well-funded citizen advisory group can help to protect the environment in all of its stages.

At Prince William Sound RCAC, we have learned that the best way to resolve contentious issues is with solid science and technical analysis, and through a partnership approach. We hire expert consultants to make the scientific, engineering, or technical case for our position, and we include industry representatives in the process at all stages. In the end we have a result that works for all parties. Many times, the industry ends up highlighting these outcomes in advertisements touting its proactive concern for environmental protection. The critical two elements in any successful citizen organization are adequate funding and independence.

One reason the Oil Pollution Act called for the creation of citizens' councils was the need to improve trust between the public, the oil industry, and government regulators. The post-*Exxon Valdez* era has seen great strides in that direction. We at the Prince William Sound RCAC look forward to continuing and strengthening this crucial relationship in years to come so that future generations never have to learn first-hand what Alaskans experienced in 1989.

Meeting the Environmental Challenge in the North Aleutian Basin: Audience Questions and Answers

Q: Does climate change research play a role for carrying out environmental impact assessments?

JON KURLAND: Yes. The Alaska Fisheries Science Center's research is focusing a lot on loss of sea ice and climate change. However, we have an incomplete understanding of the natural interannual variability of the ecosystem. This makes it difficult to understand potential changes in addition to development, due to the number of variables.

Q: Prince William Sound has been successful at obtaining financing for the citizen's advisory council, but only after a major catastrophe. How can a community negotiate long-term financing or an agreement before a major catastrophe?

JOHN DEVENS: Now would be the time for the citizens to organize and reach an agreement with industry. Municipalities can tax industry and there are a number of ways to finance it. We were lucky in that the world was upset over the *Exxon Valdez* oil spill, so there was a lot of pressure. Initially, they guaranteed $2 million a year based on the cost of living increase. Over the years it's gone up, and I think we're at $2.8 million, but the rest of the budget is from grants and contracts.

Q: Are you aware of your office's letter to the North Pacific Research Board (NPRB), which challenged the research methods for habitat protection in the Bering Sea?

JON KURLAND: That letter asked NPRB to consider a workshop to identify the research questions in regard to the habitat function of the Bering Sea canyons before providing significant funding for research. My understanding is that NPRB didn't receive any specific proposals for research in those areas. My impression is they've taken our recommendation under consideration for the future.

Q: Are there any other regions of salmon that use the lease area besides the Bristol Bay stocks?

BOB MURPHY: North Peninsula stocks are in the area. I believe the Arctic, Yukon, and Kuskokwim would be present as well. They have recovered Kodiak salmon in the Bering Sea. They also have Cook Inlet fish out there, as well as Russian and Japanese salmon stocks.

Q: Would you identify any one area in the world where you think it is worth the risk to develop oil and gas?

KELLY HARRELL: My organization does not have a position on whether oil and gas development is acceptable in other places in the world. Our position on Bristol Bay is that the risks are too great.

BUBBA COOK: It's specific to the individual location and how the operations proceed forward. There's certainly a possibility that onshore oil and gas development may have minimal impacts, but our position is that the Arctic should be off limits.

Q: You indicated that now is the time for the regional citizens advisory council (RCAC) process to begin. Who should fund the RCAC?

JOHN DEVENS: The first step is to create an organization. Talk with your congressional delegation about securing funding into the Oil Pollution Act of 1990 (OPA 90). This would give your organization a legal standing. At Prince William Sound RCAC, we have a certain legal standing when dealing with federal agencies, because they are required by OPA 90 to consult with us when making decisions about oil transportation. We are also permitted access to records that other organizations may not be able to access. The Prince William Sound RCAC started when Rick Steiner and other Cordova citizens decided that a citizens' advisory group should be formed long before an oil spill occurs. Nothing really happened until we had the spill. It seems foolish to me not to start moving in that direction, and the first step is to get organized. I'm here to encourage you to start looking at it and get something in place.

Q: I have a question for the Alaska Department of Fish and Game. Why is your presentation focused entirely on the North Alaska Peninsula and not on the fisheries in the northern part of Bristol Bay? Do you think that the fisheries in the North Alaska Peninsula are threatened and need exceptional care?

BOB MURPHY: I'm the area biologist at Port Moller. When the proceedings of the symposium came out, we realized there wasn't much discussion on the North Alaska Peninsula, so that's why I focused on that area. The north peninsula fisheries are not stressed. Right now we have healthy fisheries.

Q: We are organizing the Bristol Bay region, so it's not as though we're standing in the corner with our hands over our eyes and ears waiting for the next spill. In the last few years I've organized meetings where we have met with industry and the University of Alaska. As a matter of fact, Alaska Sea Grant has assisted with the planning stages of this meeting. We've gotten everyone involved to be sure that we are getting our ducks in a row. Last year, we decided to plan an Outer Continental Shelf (OCS) indigenous peoples movement.

Do any of the precautions associated with offshore oil development encourage NOAA to become involved with the lease sale?

JON KURLAND: NOAA doesn't have the authority to regulate oil and gas development, but we would certainly be involved in the environmental review process, commenting on the effects on fish and marine mammals.

JOHN DEVENS: That is encouraging. Now is the time to start training for the people who live in the region. Look at the experience Sakhalin Island had with industry. The community's expectations were that the economy would be stimulated. It's my understanding that most of the stimulation took place in New Zealand and Australia because that is where the food products were shipped from.

Q: One of you mentioned the Bristol Bay area plan, so I looked it up and I'm going to read a little bit from it. It says the Alaska Department of Natural Resources (DNR) and the Lake and Peninsula, Bristol Bay, and the Aleutians East boroughs have signed a memorandum of understanding (MOA) in support of oil and gas lease sales and licensing of state land in Bristol Bay and Alaska Peninsula regions. Similar MOAs are in effect between the DNR and the Aleut Regional Native Corporation, and between the DNR and Bristol Bay Native Corporation. This question is for World Wildlife Fund (WWF) and Alaska Marine Conservation Council (AMCC) representatives. Have you incorporated local input into your positions?

KELLY HARRELL: Yes, AMCC has certainly incorporated that MOU and the local support for onshore development into our position. We do not have a position on onshore development. The local people seem to support it and that's where it should move forward.

Q: Just to be clear, those organizations only represent part of the interest in those areas. We spent a significant degree of time visiting with people in Dillingham and other communities and gauging their interest and needs. We certainly take into account that there are economic hardships in the area, but we think that they would be addressed better through other measures than the proposed offshore oil and gas development.

Q: I think I heard you say that hurricanes produce 60 mile per hour winds when approaching shore. Just to clarify for the audience, a hurricane loses power when it hits the coastline. When damage occurred in hurricanes offshore, winds were sustained at 170 miles an hour with gusts 25 up to 250 miles an hour. You showed some dramatic pictures of tanker spills—*Exxon Valdez*, a spill in Korea, a tanker loading accident in the North Sea—none of which is proposed for the Bering Sea that I am aware of. You said that you have witnessed fishery decline in conjunction with oil and gas development. Fishermen's data from Cook Inlet and the sockeye salmon fishery suggest the fishery is as good as it's ever been.

BUBBA COOK: Looking at the general picture of fisheries across the globe, there is a correlation between industrial development related to oil and gas development and declining fisheries. I think it's something that should be considered in relationship to the development that's proposed in Bristol Bay.

Q: Why did you suggest to us that the Sullom Voe Association was the way to go and John suggested the RCAC?

JOHN DEVENS: Jonathan Wills of Sullom Voe really thinks that RCAC is the way to go, that our RCAC does more to protect the environment. I think you need both. I'm impressed that the Sullom Voe Association was proactive and funded local needs. RCAC does a lot more than Sullom Voe in terms of protecting the environment. I remember a conversation I had with Ted Stevens back in 1989. Senator Stevens said that despite similar goals, local citizens' priorities are different from the state or the federal government or the industry's priorities. You need to decide what you want, and do something about it without depending on those entities.

Concerns and Issues from the Fishing Industry

Concerns and Issues from the Fishing Industry: Introduction to the Panel

Jeff Stephan, Manager
United Fishermen's Marketing Association, Kodiak, Alaska

I would like to recognize the Alaska Sea Grant College Program, the University of Alaska, the University of Alaska Fairbanks (UAF), and the UAF School of Fisheries and Ocean Sciences for investing their attention, good offices, and resources, including their dedicated and hardworking staff, to convene this workshop.

Alaska Sea Grant, and its director Brian Allee, deserve special recognition for their monumental effort and valuable contribution to facilitate and organize this workshop, and for advancing the process that is under way to identify concerns, issues, opportunities, costs, and benefits of the federal oil and gas lease sales that are under consideration in the North Aleutian Basin. Alaska Sea Grant has gone to great lengths to identify a broad and diverse cross section of influential, interested, and affected parties, and to invite their participation.

Preface

Exploration, development, and extraction of the oil and gas resources of the outer continental shelf (OCS), including the North Aleutian Basin, is largely governed through an established regulatory process managed by the Minerals Management Service (MMS) of the U.S. Department of the Interior. This regulatory process is designed to invite and assimilate participation and comment from the public, and from the scientific, environmental and industry communities, to determine whether and to what extent this activity will be permitted, and, if permitted, to determine the details of the regulatory, permitting, and accountability regime that will govern the proposed activity.

The prospect of exploration, development, and extraction of oil and gas resources in the North Aleutian Basin raises legitimate concerns, issues, and awareness with respect to the complex and dynamic resource, ecosystem, social, economic, and cultural characteristics that are impacted by the proposed activities.

This workshop, while not a formal requirement of the regulatory process, is an important enhancement of the process that can only serve to expand the opportunities for improved and broader communication, participation, information, informed decision-making, and a general understanding of the opportunities, benefits, costs, and impacts of the proposed activities. This workshop is an especially important service to the public, many of whom may not otherwise have had the opportunity to be exposed to the diverse panelists and speakers, and to the associated rich and rigorous education, information, understanding, enlightenment, public interaction, and dialogue that is afforded by this event.

Commercial fishing industry

The Alaska commercial fishing industry is an important part of the equation and knowledge base that informs the feasibility of the proposed activity. We have a diverse, multidimensional, and extensive investment, interest, and commitment in the North Aleutian Basin, and we share the interest to develop an accurate and careful understanding of the impacts and opportunities that are both anticipated and unanticipated with respect to the proposed lease sales.

The Alaska commercial fishing industry has distinguished itself with having a vision, mission, and perspective that generally looks beyond the operational and management mechanisms directly associated with the catching, processing, and selling of aquatic and fisheries resources. We have demonstrated long-standing support and concern for scientific research, and for the diversity, productivity, and sustainability of the ecosystem and fisheries resources in the area of the proposed activity, and upon which we depend for our long-term survival.

The Alaska commercial fishing industry has significant standing and interest with respect to the broad time frame and diversity of activities that are associated with the proposed lease sales in the North Aleutian Basin. If we act responsibly, we can inform this decision-making process in a way that no other scientific, environmental, or industry can.

I have been the manager of the United Fishermen's Marketing Association (UFMA) in Kodiak, Alaska, for 30 years. UFMA is a trade association that is much like the Alaska Crab Coalition and United Catcher Boats. We work in the areas of regulatory and governmental affairs; marketing of Alaska seafood; coastal, marine and ocean resource management and policy; and research advocacy.

UFMA represents harvesters who utilize pot gear to harvest crab and Pacific cod in the Bering Sea/Aleutian Islands (BSAI) and Gulf of Alaska (GOA), who use hook-and-line gear to harvest halibut and sable-fish (black cod) in the BSAI and GOA, and who use seine gear to harvest salmon in the Kodiak Management Area.

Acquired perspectives and experience

Prior experiences with issues that relate to the exploration, develop-ment, and extraction of oil and gas resources in the OCS have provided me with some ability to understand, examine, and evaluate the federal oil and gas lease sales that are proposed in the North Aleutian Basin.

I was privileged to serve on the Department of the Interior OCS Policy Committee under three U.S. Secretaries of Interior during a time that reflected a policy of very aggressive development of OCS oil and gas resources. The OCS Policy Committee provides advice to the Secretary of the Interior on issues related to implementing the OCS Lands Act. My participation on the OCS Policy Committee provided me with a valuable understanding and insight with respect to the politics, science, and the varied national, public, commercial, and resource interests that are impacted by OCS oil and gas activity. I gained a great respect for the complexity of issues that impact oil and gas resource development in the OCS, the importance of investment in relevant research, and the diversity of concerns that address conservation, environmental, com-munity, social, cultural, and commercial interests. I also gained great respect for the roles and responsibilities of the MMS and the states; they have a difficult, costly, and complex responsibility.

I traveled to Norway with a small group of Alaskans in 1980 as a guest of the Norwegian government. We visited Oslo, Trondheim, Bergen, the Lofoten Islands, Tromsø, and other regions. Our main mission was to become familiar with the technology, processing, harvesting, marketing, and other successes of the Norwegian fishing industry, and to examine potential partnerships with Norwegian commercial fishing enterprises. We also received a heavy dose of education about the oil and gas devel-opment in offshore Norwegian waters, and about the interaction among representatives of the public, environmental, governmental, commercial fishing, and oil and gas interests. My eyes were opened with respect to the benefits to commerce, the environment, and the national and public interest that are possible when a nation invests its education and research toward understanding and mitigating the risks and maximiz-ing the opportunities of oil and gas development offshore.

I became involved in March 1989 with organizing the initial Kodiak management and response strategy to address the *Exxon Valdez* oil spill. People in the Kodiak community, including UFMA members, were very concerned about the impacts of the spill on Kodiak's fisheries, the habitat in which these resources live and reproduce, and other natural, cultural, human, and commercial assets.

I had previously been involved in the process of federal oil and gas lease sales, and other exploration and development activities in the Gulf of Alaska. As part of that experience, I became familiar with the literature that addressed the coastal current and ocean circulation patterns along the Alaska coast. As part of that understanding, and the knowledge gained on the OCS Advisory Committee, it was clear to me that Kodiak was in the trajectory of *Exxon Valdez* oil, and that our assets were at risk. Our challenge was in convincing senior Exxon representatives and our local governments that Kodiak was at risk, and that we had no more than two weeks before we were to feel the impact of the spilled oil.

I would like to recognize the scientists, especially those at the University of Alaska Fairbanks, for their important work to advance the study of the coastal current and ocean circulation patterns in the Gulf of Alaska. Their work helped us anticipate, with a high degree of certainty, and in the face of some official skepticism, that the spilled oil was coming to Kodiak. Specifically, I would like to recognize Dr. Tom Royer, a UAF professor for many years, who was one of the first to design and lead research on Gulf of Alaska currents and ocean circulation. Immediately after the *Exxon Valdez* incident we consulted Dr. Royer, and he provided valuable and important confirmation of our concerns.

I would like to recognize many of the Exxon employees with whom we worked during the Kodiak response to the spill, who held leadership and field responsibility for Kodiak-related issues during the spill; they were helpful, professional, and responsive to our needs and suggestions.

I would like also to recognize Alaska Governor Steve Cowper and Alaska Commissioner of Environmental Conservation Dennis Kelso for their support, attention, and perseverance on behalf of the State of Alaska, and its people, resources, and commerce during the time of the *Exxon Valdez* incident.

In the late 1970s Chevron notified us that they were planning to conduct seismic and exploration work in the Northern Shelikof Strait. UFMA and others in the community were very concerned about the many risks that seismic and platform-based exploration activity would pose there. We were concerned about the impact of the proposed activity on the crab and fishery resources, on crab gear, on harvesting activities, on marine mammal populations, and on essential habitat. We worked with Chevron to establish a structure of consultation and engagement for us to express our concerns, understand the details of the proposed activity, permit Chevron to convey their operational needs, and provide a forum where options for cooperation and problem solving were discussed. Through this engagement, we developed a strategy that accommodated our operational needs, and gave us confidence with respect to our concerns about resources and habitat. I would like to recognize Tom Cook, who was then a geologist at the Alaska Chevron office, and Tom Gallagher, who worked in governmental affairs for Chevron, and later for Sohio and British Petroleum, for their leadership and dedication to working with us to develop an avenue of consultation, and to find reasonable solutions.

Representatives of UFMA later worked with representatives of Chevron and Sohio to develop an organization that was to become known as the Oil/Fisheries Group of Alaska. The Oil/Fisheries Group of Alaska brought together representatives of the commercial fishing, seismic, and oil and gas sectors, and was intended to offer a forum for communication between these groups. We collaborated on the development of a manual that was published by the Oil/Fisheries Group of Alaska entitled *A Manual for Geophysical Operations in Fishing Areas of Alaska*. This manual provided operational information about the commercial fishing, seismic, and oil and gas industries. I would again like to recognize the work of Peter Hanley and Roger Herrera of Sohio, and Tom Cook of Chevron, for their vision, imagination, dedication, and hard work to create this organization and publication.

Lessons learned

The previously described and other experiences have provided me with some lessons and insights that assist me in looking at the multidimensional issues related to the exploration, development, and extraction of oil and gas in the OCS.

I learned that people are important and central to understanding and problem solving. I have purposely recognized a few individuals to illustrate this point. There are many people of good will in the scientific community, agencies, oil and gas industry, fishing industry, environmental community, etc., who can and should come together in a spirit of intellectual curiosity to rigorously address their diverse perspectives and concerns to deal with the many issues associated with OCS oil and gas activity.

I learned that rigorous, penetrating, honest, and forthright engagement and communication is very important in addressing the challenges of OCS oil and gas activity.

I learned, as most of you already know, that while planning is important, the plan is not always as fruitful and important as the planning process, or as important as the discussions, enlightenment, and collaboration that accompany the planning process.

I learned that while it is important to make every effort to develop a comprehensive list of concerns, threats, risks, and opportunities, and to do the hard work to identify the gaps, and to try to fill those gaps, it is equally important to recognize that the unidentified and unanticipated consequences can be those that have most long-lasting impact on the numerous resource, environmental, cultural, community, and commercial considerations that must be addressed.

I learned that the agencies have the authority and responsibility to establish the regulations, guidelines, and other mechanisms that govern the exploration, development, and extraction of oil and gas resources in critical areas.

I learned that the oil and gas industry has significant influence in the agencies, and with the elected and appointed officials who have the authority and responsibility to establish or influence the regulations, guidelines, and other mechanisms that govern the exploration, development, and extraction of oil and gas resources in critical areas.

I learned that the agencies sometimes have a tendency to believe and act in a manner that conveys the attitude that they possess the most important and relevant knowledge, perspectives, information, understandings, solutions, and processes.

I learned that it is occasionally evident that the oil and gas industry has, to me, a discomforting influence with some elements of the scientific and academic community.

I learned that it is the responsibility of the public to engage in the decision-making process in a manner that is reasonable, informed, and thoughtful, to hold the responsible agencies accountable for their decisions with respect to mechanisms that permit and govern oil and gas activities in the OCS, and to demand ongoing oversight by the agencies to monitor the permitted activities.

I learned that partnerships, associations, and other similar efforts that seek and facilitate knowledge and understanding, and that are sometimes meant to bring disparate entities together, are very important.

I learned that universities can play, and should play, a critical and important role in facilitating, but not leading, those partnerships and associations.

I learned that the universities should have an important role in leading, promoting, designing, and executing the scientific, social, and economic research that examines and identifies the parameters, impacts, costs, and benefits of those activities that are anticipated with respect to OCS oil and gas activity.

I learned that Alaska coastal residents, while they are likely to be variably impacted by the benefits of oil and gas activity in the OCS, are also likely to be the most impacted by the costs and failures of these activities.

I learned that a decision to prohibit oil and gas activity in some areas can be justified and well founded at specific times, but that such decisions should also be subject to review and revision as technology, information, and other circumstances change.

The proposition

It is reasonable and proper that an initiative to explore, develop, and extract oil and gas in an area that has such ecological and established cultural and commercial significance and characteristics as the North Aleutian Basin should have a thorough and penetrating review. It is fitting that the Alaska commercial fishing industry can and should have a significant involvement and impact in evaluating and informing the feasibility and parameters of such proposed activity.

Now, to the panel discussion.

Alaska Crab Coalition Perspective and Concerns Regarding North Aleutian Basin OCS Development

Arni Thomson, Executive Director
Alaska Crab Coalition, Seattle, Washington

The Alaska Crab Coalition (ACC) is aware of the 40-year history of coexistence between fisheries and gas and oil production in the Gulf of Mexico, Cook Inlet, Eastern Canada, and Norway. Last May I was provided the opportunity to participate in a two-day seminar in Henningsvaer, Lofoten, Norway where I was exposed to the realities of coexistence and the latest Norwegian gas and oil sub-seabed directional drilling and extraction technology in arctic offshore areas. Such technology can minimize the footprint in sensitive benthic habitat and it can also provide assurances of environmental protection for our abundant fisheries of the southeastern Bering Sea and Bristol Bay.

Environmental and fisheries protections are the major priority of the ACC. Alaska coastal communities and other fishermen and processors are economically dependent on this region for sustainable production of fisheries resources. Despite the risks and challenges facing environmentally sound OCS development in this area, the need to engage in the dialogue here today is very strong. OCS development with the potential for long-term jobs and careers can help deter the outmigration of families and youth from the coastal communities of the Alaska Peninsula and the Bristol Bay area, occurring now as a result of declining income in traditional fisheries. The ACC also recognizes that North Aleutian Basin exploration and development can be a part of a national agenda to reduce dependence on foreign gas and oil resources.

There are inherent challenges for fisheries and OCS coexistence in the North Aleutian Basin, as shown in Figures 1-6. The current 2007-2008 ex-vessel value of the king, *Chionoecetes bairdi*, and snow crab fisheries is in excess of $180 million.

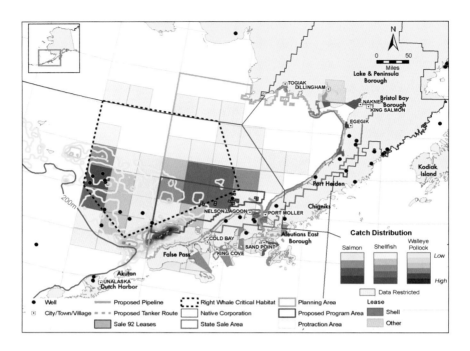

Figure 1. **Map showing locations for the proposed lease area, oil interests, important fisheries, North Pacific right whale critical habitat, proposed pipeline and tanker route, etc., in the North Aleutian Basin, Alaska. Source: Shell Exploration and Production Company.**

The ACC has concerns it would like to see addressed:

1. The ACC supports the Aleutians East Borough/Lake and Peninsula Borough Memorandum of Understanding and Proposed Mitigation Measures for OCS Development in the North Aleutian Basin Planning Area.

2. The ACC would like to see a clear description of the scope and size of oil and gas installations and what limitations they pose for fisheries; impacts and restrictions from seismic activity; discharges; gas and oil spill response and mitigation plans, developed in consort with a regional advisory council; timely compensation to the fishing industry and coastal communities in the event of disruption of fisheries; and research on the potential impacts to seafood markets, in light of the Alaska Seafood Marketing Institute message that "Alaska seafood is wild, sustainable and harvested in the pristine waters off the coast of Alaska."

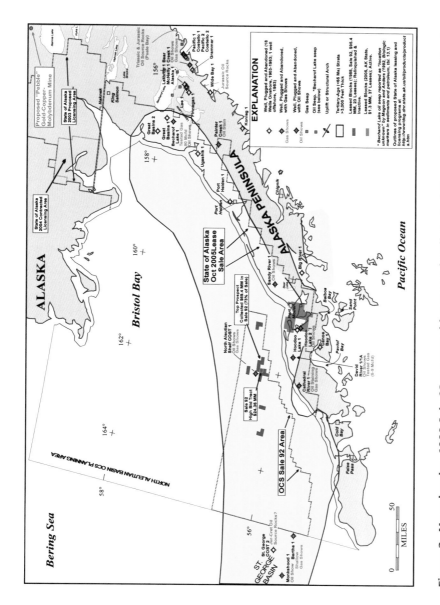

Figure 2. Map showing 1988 Sale 92 proposed leases and well control. Source: North Aleutian Basin OCS Planning Area, U.S. Dept. of Interior, MMS, 2006, p. 92.

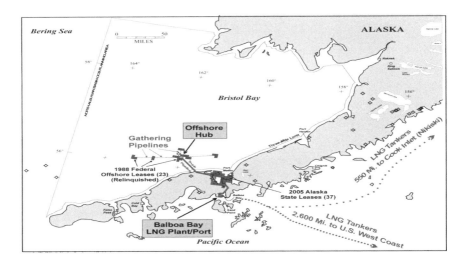

Figure 3. Map showing a hypothetical development model for North Aleutian basin gas resources. North Aleutian Basin OCS Planning Area, U.S. Dept. of Interior, MMS, 2006, p. 138.

3. The ACC would like to see a commitment from industry and the federal government to develop and implement a long-term scientific monitoring program to assess potential impacts to the marine environment and the fisheries and marine resources of the North Aleutian Basin.

4. The ACC would also like to see a discussion of commitments from potential leaseholders on environmental protection of fisheries and marine resources, fisheries compensation, commitments to the Tri-Borough Mitigation Measures, and funding in whole or in part of scientific monitoring systems and other research data needs defined by the Steering Committee.

5. Overall, in the event of OCS development in the North Aleutian Basin, the ACC would like to see policies of conflict avoidance and mutual respect for shared access to the resources. To achieve this requires negotiated compromises. All or most of the fisheries' sectors represented here today, commercial, subsistence, sport, recreational and conservation groups are well acquainted with the public processes and risk assessment negotiations associated with the Alaska Board of Fisheries and the North Pacific Fishery Management Council. The process is seldom easy and it can become highly charged when a new user group enters a fisheries region.

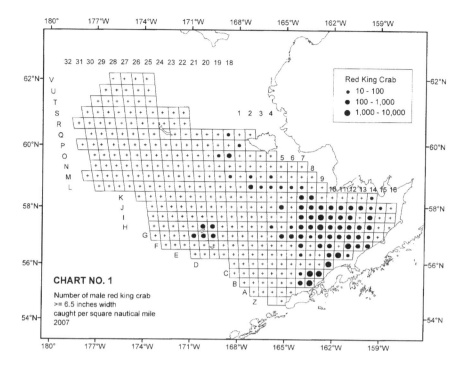

Figure 4. Number of female red king crab caught per square nautical mile in the southeastern Bering Sea, 2007. Source: Preliminary Results: 2007 Eastern Bering Sea Trawl Survey, NMFS, RACE Shellfish Assessment Program.

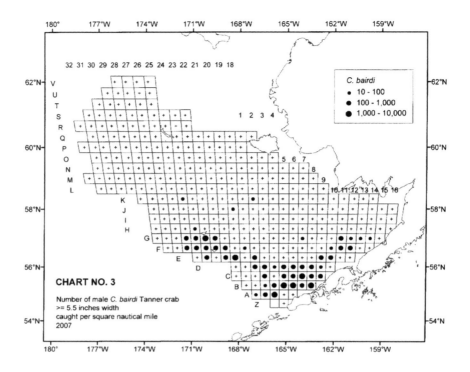

Figure 5. Number of male *Chionoecetes bairdi* Tanner crab caught per square nautical mile in the southeastern Bering Sea, 2007. Source: Preliminary Results: 2007 Eastern Bering Sea Trawl Survey, NMFS, RACE Shellfish Assessment Program.

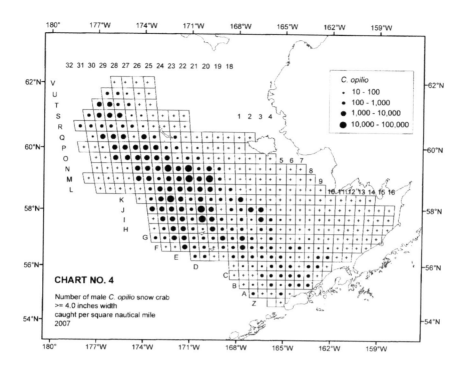

Figure 6. Number of male *Chionoecetes opilio* snow crab caught per square nautical mile in the southeastern Bering Sea, 2007. Source: Preliminary Results: 2007 Eastern Bering Sea Trawl Survey, NMFS, RACE Shellfish Assessment Program.

North Aleutian Basin Oil and Gas: Fishery Industry Concerns

Brent Paine, Director
United Catcher Boats, Seattle, Washington

I will talk about United Catcher Boats and what we do, characteristics of the eastern Bering Sea pollock fleet and other fisheries that we're involved with, the value of the fisheries, how the fishing industry can participate in the issue of the North Aleutian Basin oil and gas lease sale, and the concerns we might have about a lease sale in the North Aleutian Basin.

Eastern Bering Sea fisheries

United Catcher Boats represents about 67 trawl catcher vessels participating in the North Pacific groundfish and crab fisheries. The eastern Bering Sea fishery is trawl, longline, and pot vessels that have been fishing in the eastern Bering Sea since the 1940s or 1950s. The Magnuson Act, enacted in the mid 1970s, was the impetus for the development of the fleet that is in the eastern Bering Sea and the Gulf of Alaska today.

About 120 trawl catcher vessels fish in the eastern Bering Sea. There are about 40 trawl catcher processors; of those catcher processors about a dozen fish for pollock with pelagic gear and the remainder fish with bottom trawl gear for species such as yellowfin sole, flathead sole, Atka mackerel, and cod. The catcher vessels fish primarily with pelagic gear for pollock. They also fish with bottom trawl gear, for species like Pacific cod and yellowfin sole. In 2006 there were about 30 longline catcher processors and 150 pot catcher vessels. Probably because of rationalization of the crab fisheries they have dropped to about 50 active vessels.

The 2006 total ex-vessel value of groundfish fisheries was $753 million, at 2.2 million tons. The eastern Bering Sea pollock fishery alone is worth about $200 million. If you add the first wholesale value price of pollock, upwards of $800 million is coming out of the eastern Bering Sea annually.

The single largest fishery in the world is the eastern Bering Sea pollock fishery. That's just one of the gems we have that is currently sustainable and renewable. And it's growing amazingly—the price for groundfish products in the next decade is probably going to double, or more than double, because of the demand for protein that comes from the ocean.

The total 2006 ex-vessel value of the eastern Bering Sea crab fisheries was roughly $80 million. According to Arni Thomson, because of the rebuilding of the snow crab fishery, it's now about $150 million a year. And it's been much higher than that in previous years.

Fisheries and the North Aleutian Basin proposed lease area

A large number of fisheries occur inside the proposed North Aleutian Basin lease area—pollock, Pacific cod, flatfish, etc. For the 2005 pollock fishery, 21%, or about 317,000 tons of fish, were harvested out of the area in which the lease sale would occur. The commercial red king crab fishery overlaps almost exactly with the lease sale area.

In terms of the environmental concerns for the people and the boats that I work for, the effect of oil and gas development on essential fish habitat within the North Aleutian Basin is one of the key issues for us. I grew up in Homer, and I remember clearly the battle over Kachemak Bay oil leases, which the State of Alaska had let and then bought back. I don't think oil and gas drilling would be a good mix with what Kachemak Bay provides for the people who live in Homer. However, central Cook Inlet seems like an appropriate place—the way those fields have been developed works well. We have a billion dollar fishery in the North Aleutian Basin. If we put on top of that an oil and gas production industry, it could be difficult. It might be possible, but it seems like the stakeholders who are involved in the fishery right now would be put at risk.

The North Aleutian Basin is essential fish habitat. The reason that it's the largest fishery in the world is that the eastern Bering Sea shelf has one of the most active upwelling systems in the world. It's a very dynamic, very productive ecosystem. For example, more than 20 species of fish depend on the ecosystem in this area for all their life history stages.

Potential impacts to the fisheries

The specific impacts to the fishing industry that we're concerned about are first, seismic surveys. What impact does that kind of acoustic pressure signal have on fish and crab? And secondly, what kind of conflict is there between the gears that are out there? If the vessels that I work for are fishing for pollock and come in contact with a seismic vessel, that's a potential problem. We need to think about how we can mitigate that.

Also of concern are the impacts of drilling rig locations within the core fishing areas. A pelagic trawl fishery and bottom trawl fishery are mobile—we tow for four to six hours. What happens if we're towing up a school of fish and there's a drilling rig in front of us? We need to think about those kinds of interactions before we start going forward.

Ocean floor pipelines—what happens if a cod trawl on the bottom comes across a pipeline? Is that a problem? It is likely that the development of an environmental impact statement and the proper public process will answer some of these questions, but right now we don't know.

Last are the impacts of tanker transportation of oil and gas. We all know the fate of salmon and herring fishermen in Prince William Sound who faced a tanker disaster. And what happens if there is a blowout? The Prince William Sound herring fishery still doesn't exist today, many years later after the *Exxon Valdez* oil spill. The fishermen are waiting for a Supreme Court decision, whether the punitive damages are going to be awarded or not.

Compensation mechanism

My last point is a compensation mechanism for loss. The pollock fishery is worth $200 million a year, about 200 times greater than the herring fishery in Prince William Sound. Would the Shell Oil Company be willing to go to an underwriter and establish a contingency fund to guarantee the fishing fleet the value lost because of a biological disaster, such as an oil spill or problems with the development of oil and gas in the eastern Bering Sea? If they were to say yes, then I think my members would be a little bit more receptive to this kind of a development proposal.

It's not only the value of the lost fishery—it's also the value of the market. We have spent many, many years since the development of the domestic fishery in the United States, with the passage of the Magnuson Act in the 1970s, developing high quality Alaska fish products marketed internationally and domestically. If it gets tainted by an environmental disaster, it seems that the work done by ASMI (Alaska Seafood Marketing Institute) and the industry would be for naught. It's a concern that we want to put out there.

"Zoning" for fisheries and energy development

The North Pacific Fishery Management Council has been very proactive in developing conservation management measures that govern the Bering Sea/Aleutian Islands and Gulf of Alaska fisheries. They have put essential fish habitat regulations into effect based on the Magnuson Act amendments enacted about 12 years ago. This zoning approach to fishery management says that if habitat areas need protection, they will be closed to fishing.

For fishermen, closure to fishing actually provides a more productive, more sustainable system. For the environment it provides protection for key life history stages of the fish in that habitat. It has been a win/win situation. The fishermen were supportive, but grudgingly, of this kind of management measure. And now there are hundreds of thousands of acres closed to fishing in the eastern Bering Sea/Aleutian Islands, and some in the Gulf of Alaska, because of this type of a management program. A similar zoning approach could be considered for the oil and gas industry. Oil and gas and mineral management are all new to me, but when we develop a city, etc., we talk about zoning for different kinds of building. Maybe the areas in the eastern Bering Sea that are more valuable could be zoned to not allow oil and gas development. For example, oil and gas development works in the West Foreland Field and Cook Inlet, but would not work in Kachemak Bay.

Conclusion

I want to close by posing a couple of questions. (1) Why should the current users of the Bering Sea resource incur risk to their activities from new oil and gas development? Nowhere else in the world are the stakes so high. (2) Why should current users who have paid a high price and supplied a litany of management measures to protect the resource incur risk by a new user group? The North Pacific fisheries have been managed with a precautionary approach, and that precautionary approach should also apply to the oil and gas industry. Thank you very much.

Energy Development and Healthy Fisheries

Dale Schwarzmiller
Peter Pan Seafoods, Seattle, Washington

Peter Pan Seafoods has a long history with the people, communities, and resources of the Alaska Peninsula region and the Bristol Bay region. We process crab, cod, pollock, salmon, halibut, herring, and blackcod at our King Cove plant, and salmon production is very important to us at our Dillingham facility and at our Port Moller plant. Our success here is directly dependent on healthy fisheries and the viability of local communities.

Some level of energy development in this region would go a long way toward diversifying the economies of the region, as well as providing needed jobs and infrastructure. Recent history in Alaska and other regions in the world have shown that energy development and fisheries can successfully coexist. While we are optimistic that outer continental shelf development can be a positive step to reduce dependence on foreign oil and gas resources and be of benefit to the local economy, we share the concerns of many that such development be done only if mitigation measures are in place after a transparent review and approval process. Peter Pan would like to be part of that review process.

We support the Aleutians East Borough's proposed mitigation measures for OCS leasing in the North Aleutian Basin. I will summarize from their document and add comments specific to our company point of view.

Regarding fisheries protection, quoting from the Aleutians East Borough's document, "Lease-related use will be restricted to prevent conflicts with local, commercial, subsistence, and sport harvest activities. All OCS operations both on shore and offshore must be designed, sited, and operated to ensure that (1) adverse changes to the distribution or abundance of fish resources do not occur; (2) fish or shellfish catches are not adversely impacted by OCS activities, (3) all exploration, construction, and operation activities will be coordinated with the fishing community to maximize communication, ensure public participation, and avoid conflicts; (4) ballast water treatment is required to remove or eliminate nonindigenous species; (5) fishermen are not displaced or precluded from access to fishing areas unless they are adequately compensated for the displacement; (6) fishermen are not precluded from participating in designated fishing seasons unless they are adequately compensated for the lost seasons; and (7) fishermen will be compensated for damage to fishing equipment, vessels, gear, and decreased harvest value from OCS operations in a timely manner."

In addition to the fishery protection issues, Peter Pan would ask that processors also be compensated should fishermen be displaced from fishing areas or precluded from participating in designated fishing seasons due to the outcome of OCS activities. The coastal communities of Alaska include fishermen and processors and both go hand in hand. Adverse effects of OCS development could have serious impacts on both the fishing and processing sectors.

Peter Pan also supports the balance of the Aleutians East Borough proposed mitigation measures. The Aleutians East Borough document goes into detail regarding the following important issues related to OCS development: (1) federal funding should be available to conduct independent fisheries and environmental studies before any oil drilling in the area; (2) transportation, utility corridors, and infrastructure sighting must be carefully sited to allow for free passage and movement of fish and wildlife; (3) coastal habitat protection, the best available oil spill prevention and response technologies must be used and the response must be rapid; (4) local hiring and training involving planning and recruiting local contractors, businesses, and residents should be part of the program; (5) there should be provisions for local government revenue sharing; (6) the best available technology for air and water pollution control should be used; (7) marine mammals and essential habitat protection should be addressed; (8) social system protections including a provision stipulating that the OCS developers communicate with local residents, interested local community groups, and especially fishing organizations; (9) historical and cultural preservation must be addressed; and (10) seismic design must be addressed.

In conclusion, we are encouraged by the positive information we have learned through the steering committee process and through discussion with folks like the Aleutians East Borough mayor and others about coexistence of fisheries and offshore oil and gas development in places like Norway. We understand that fisheries and offshore development have successfully coexisted in Cook Inlet for several years now, and we support the process going forward, but agree that it must be done in a transparent and responsible manner. Thank you.

Concerns and Issues from the Fishing Industry—NPFMC

Eric Olson, Chair
North Pacific Fishery Management Council, Anchorage, Alaska

For this presentation I am wearing a couple of hats. First and foremost, I am lifelong commercial salmon fisherman and a Bristol Bay drift gillnet permit holder. When not fishing in Bristol Bay, I work for a company called Kwik'pak Fisheries, which buys and processes chinook and chum salmon at the mouth of the Yukon River. (As a side note, the word "Kwik'pak" is actually a Yupik word that means Big River.)

In my spare time, I serve on the North Pacific Fishery Management Council and am also the current chairman. As many of you know the North Pacific Fishery Management Council is one of eight regional councils in the United States that oversee the management of federal fisheries that occur from 3 to 200 miles off our coast.

The majority of this presentation describes the concerns from the perspective of nearshore Western Alaska fisheries. Arni Thomson, Brent Paine, and Dale Schwarzmiller are covering the crab and groundfish fisheries that occur farther from shore.

I will start off with a description of the nearshore fisheries, as well as some statistics. I apologize in advance for not having a PowerPoint to lay out this information nice and neat, but I was afraid that would put my street credibility in jeopardy with the active fishermen in the room!

Bristol Bay salmon

Bristol Bay is composed of five separate districts—Togiak, Nushagak, Naknek-Kvichak, Egegik, and Ugashik. Collectively, these five districts are home to the largest commercial sockeye salmon fishery in the world.

It is also the largest fishery in Alaska with respect to number of permit holders. Roughly 1,800 drift gillnet and 1,000 set gillnet permits are authorized to harvest salmon. In 2007 Alaska residents held about half the drift gillnet permits, and more than 60% of the set gillnet permits that fished. On average, nearly one-third of the total earnings from Alaska salmon fishing come from Bristol Bay waters.

Five species of salmon return to Bristol Bay: chinook, sockeye, chum, coho, and, on even years, pinks. Average harvests of these species from 1984 to 2003 were

> 24 million sockeye
> 971,000 chum
> 593,000 pink (even years)
> 133,000 coho
> 69,000 chinook

In 2007, according to the Alaska Department of Fish and Game, the total inshore Bristol Bay sockeye run was approximately 44.3 million fish with a commercial harvest of 29.5 million, which rank 9th and 8th respectively since statehood. The total run was 10 million more than the preseason forecast. ADFG's 2008 sockeye forecast is 40.3 million fish, with an estimated commercial harvest of 31.4 million.

The chum fishery in 2007 was approximately 2 million fish and was more than twice the 20 year average. The chinook salmon fishery was below average in 2007, with a total harvest of 63,400.

The 2007 estimated total ex-vessel value of all salmon fisheries in Bristol Bay, before post-season price adjustments, exceeded $108 million. The lion's share of that, $106 million, was attributed to the sockeye salmon fishery. The remaining $2.2 was broken out to $1.54 million for chum, $550,000 for chinook, and $100,000 for coho.

Sportfishing

With regard to sportfishing, the Bristol Bay Management Area (roughly the size of the state of Wisconsin) contains some of the most productive salmon, rainbow trout, arctic grayling, arctic char, and Dolly Varden waters in the world. A 2005 angler survey conducted by the University of Montana found that the freshwater rivers, streams, and lakes of the region are "a recreational resource equal or superior in quality to other world renowned fisheries."

Survey results consistently emphasized the importance of Bristol Bay's uncrowded, remote, and wild setting in their decisions to fish the area. In 2005, it is estimated that nonresident Alaskans made 13,000 trips and spent approximately $48 million specifically for the purpose of fishing in the Bristol Bay region. Alaska residents add an estimated $13 million for a total of $61 million.

Herring

The 2007 Togiak herring fishery harvested roughly 16,000 tons, and also had its lowest total value since the inception of the fishery. With a grounds price estimate ex-vessel value of $100 per ton, the total ex-vessel value of that fishery is $1.6 million.

4E halibut fishery

The Area 4E halibut CDQ fishery, which is harvested 100% by residents of Western Alaska, had a total harvest in 2007 of 580,000 pounds. It is the highest level of harvest on record for that fishery. At an estimated ex-vessel price of $3.00-$3.50 per pound, the total value of that fishery in 2007 is between $1.7 and $2.0 million.

Halibut and crab nurseries

In her presentation, Jane DiCosimo highlighted the important nursery grounds for halibut and red king crab. This area could be highly susceptible to potential impacts of development.

Resources are of high value

I know this panel is focused on commercial fisheries, but there are also vibrant subsistence fisheries in the area. There is also a panel on subsistence fisheries during the workshop, but I wanted to remind you that subsistence fisheries would also be affected.

What do all of these statistics show? I hope the take-home message of my presentation is that the renewable fishery resources north of the proposed development are of significant value, not only to the Bristol Bay region but to the entire state of Alaska.

The statistics presented above are just for areas around Bristol Bay. A similar description of the fisheries on the Kuskokwim, Yukon, and areas farther north could also be done. The potential impacts on these fisheries throughout Western Alaska need to be fully analyzed. Salmon headed to and from the river systems of all these regions travel through the North Aleutian Basin at various times in their life cycle.

What needs to happen if drilling is to occur

A Yes or No decision on whether drilling should occur is not going to be the outcome of this workshop. Rather this is a forum for people on all sides of this issue to identify their concerns.

Quite frankly, there is a heightened level of concern by the fishermen of Western Alaska, and the burden of proof that potential development in the North Aleutian Basin will not negatively affect the region's fisheries economy will be very challenging.

If drilling is to occur, at a minimum I feel there needs to be

1. A full understanding of the potential impacts to the habitat of the area and the effects on the fisheries resources.

2. A first class disaster prevention system put in place. The value of the state and federal fisheries in this area necessitate proactive prevention measures.

3. Very stringent mitigation measures planned and ready to go in the event of a spill.

4. All phases of the development conducted in a manner that will reduce conflicts with fishing activity and fisheries resources.

In closing, I'd like to ask that you think about how you put a value on the future of a fishery that could be affected by, heaven forbid, a large scale spill in this region. I'm sure there are economists out there who can do it, and there may be a few in this room. But I think if you ask the people who live in this region and participate in these fisheries, many would respond in a similar fashion to that old MasterCard commercial: Priceless!

I appreciate the opportunity to speak today and look forward to an open dialogue and discussion on this issue in the future. Thank you.

Concerns and Issues from the Fishing Industry: Audience Questions and Answers

Q: Eric, I'm proud of you and you did a good presentation. You represented this Bristol Bay very well. I'd like to mention that a large percentage of the fishermen in Bristol Bay are from outside Alaska. They would be impacted also.

ERIC OLSON: Yes, thank you for pointing that out. There are many fishermen from Washington and Oregon. I even saw a boat from Florida a couple of summers ago. People from all over the world participate in this fishery.

Q: For the Bristol Bay and the Bering Sea region, no other industry has surpassed the amount of employment income of the commercial fishery since it first started. The canneries are all offshore. It would be good to talk more on the subsistence side.

Q: Habitat is at high risk. And the risk of an oil spill and its effect on fish stocks is high. A lot of information is available from Norway.

BRENT PAINE: I'll address that from a fisheries management perspective. We are governed by the Magnuson-Stevens Act and other federal laws. Primarily, the requirements for environmental impact statements or environmental assessment, whenever a management measure is being proposed, are going to go into effect. My hope is that the science that goes into five year reviews and applications for lease sales is as thorough as what I've seen by the National Marine Fisheries Service, in terms of the Protected Resources and Sustainable Fisheries Divisions.

I was glad to hear the NMFS representative say that they would like to work in consultation or in combination with Minerals Management Service on developing the impact statements that are necessary to study the effects on the environment of such a proposed oil and gas development.

JEFF STEPHAN: Would any other panelists like to comment? Are you saying that the potential impacts in the offshore area are not demonstrated in scientific literature?

Q: Yes.

JEFF STEPHAN: You mentioned muds and the drift from oil drilling locations. Let me express one thing that I seem to remember. During the

Exxon Valdez oil spill we had expressed concern mainly because some of us had been involved in the Outer Continental Shelf (OCS) program in the past. There was a fellow up at UAF who had done a lot of OCS studies and work on circulation in the Gulf of Alaska. We thought the drift was coming to Kodiak. While there was sheen, there was not a lot of oil visible in areas of the gulf where they anticipated it might be.

The Coast Guard went there with infrared light that penetrates below the surface. This revealed evidence of mousse, which is oil that is suspended below the surface. At the time, we were concerned because it was prime time for migrating herring and salmon smolt and returning salmon. We even hired several troll vessels to pick up a lot of the mousse below the surface.

If a spill were to happen in the Bering Sea, what effect would that have on the juvenile pollock?

JEFF STEPHAN: We'd like to have some other questions or concerns or some questions for the panelists here. We have quite an experienced and diverse group here and we'd sure like to put them to the test.

Q: I heard the concerns of the panel and I agree with many of them. My experience with some of these companies, Shell in particular, is that they will agree to your demands. Then as development proceeds, your options to stop it decrease. As we've seen with the *Exxon Valdez* oil spill, the compensation isn't exactly coming out the way people had hoped that it would.

So my question to the panel is, have you thought about the timing of this? And at what point do you conclude that these companies are not going to meet your demands, and say this is not going to work for us?

ERIC OLSON: I don't know if I'd characterize my presentation as a yes if these demands are met. I have some major concerns about this fishery. A lot of things need to happen before any development goes forward. I don't know if other panel members wanted to state their view on it.

BRENT PAINE: I'll state my view. My board of directors (United Catcher Boats) voted very clearly to oppose oil and gas development in the North Aleutian Basin. We feel that the risks to the commercial fishing industry are too great and the benefits from oil and gas development don't outweigh those risks.

It's an issue of a renewable resource versus a nonrenewable resource. Maybe if it's costing people four or five times more to heat their homes in the winter because the price of gas is so high or because Cook Inlet oil and gas run out, then that's a consideration.

If oil and gas are going to be developed out there, I would like to see the Shell Oil Company put in the value of the foregoing revenue of the Bering Sea pollock fishery. Go to Lloyd's of London and get a bond to guarantee that the people I work for don't have to be like the guys in Prince William Sound, Cook Inlet, and Kodiak who are hoping that the Supreme Court is going to vote in their favor this summer.

JEFF STEPHAN: Would anyone else on the panel like to address that?

ARNI THOMSON: As an outcome of this workshop, the Alaska Crab Coalition would like to see some discussion of commitments from potential leaseholders on environmental protection of fisheries and marine resources, fisheries compensation, commitments to the Aleutians East Borough and Lake and Peninsula Borough mitigation measures, and some discussion of funding scientific monitoring systems.

DALE SCHWARZMILLER: Peter Pan Seafoods shares similar concerns. We outlined the various items that we want to see mitigated. I think all of us want to see more concrete plans in place. I think that's what these types of conferences are about, to learn more about the process so we're assured that the types of things we're talking about will really come to pass.

JEFF STEPHAN: I think the memorandum of understanding and some of the so-called demands that people are asking for are very important. In the northern Shelikof Strait situation, as well as the *Exxon Valdez* oil spill, we were assured that if anything happened there were sufficient boom, sufficient mechanized equipment, and staged boats. We also had assurances from the Coast Guard. I think everyone had the best intentions and thought they were adequately prepared.

We found out with *Exxon Valdez* that there wasn't any boom anywhere, and there wasn't even equipment to operate the boom. The compensation that the fishermen got was from the interim claims settlement that we actually negotiated with Exxon. Thank goodness we did that. We moved a lot of money across the table prior to this whole thing because some of us anticipated this.

Q: I agree. There are certain things we can do as an agency under our laws and regulations, but there are other things that our lawyers say we can't. Through this dialogue we are identifying some of these issues and we're going to continue to work with crews to see if there are other methods of getting what people are looking for. Exactly how we're going to do that, I don't know yet. That's what we'll be doing over the next year or two.

SAM COTTEN: First of all, what's this going to do for the price of red salmon? What do we get out of this except a lot of risk? Have you thought about what investments in infrastructure would be helpful to the industry from the perspective of marketing or transportation—fuel costs, safety, rescue issues, and additional response equipment—that might be available for things other than oil spills? Have you seen anything that's possibly in it for you that you might be able to negotiate with the industry?

ERIC OLSON: Of your list, the only one that potentially could be a benefit is increased distribution of fuel from the northern part of Bristol Bay. I think that's quite a ways away from the proposed development. I don't see any safety benefits there. A lot of folks I talked to see nothing but risk. A certain segment of folks are worried that they're potentially going to be impacted from the south from this proposed oil development, and in the north from Pebble Mine. I don't see a lot of upside with the exception of the potential of increased fuel coming to the area.

Q: What is the methodology for prioritizing between a world-class fishery and potentially world-class gas, oil, and mining reserves? How do you make that prioritization? Is it sustainability, value, average wages, Alaskan hire, or taxes paid?

BRENT PAINE: I'll answer that. You're asking the wrong question. The question should be, what is the impact of oil and gas development on existing users and why is it their burden to figure out what the priority should be?

Secondly, I would say that a renewable resource has a higher priority than a nonrenewable resource.

Q: I think it's important as Alaskans and as Americans that we take those thoughts into consideration.

ERIC OLSON: I recognize your point. Although fishermen are struggling with the cost of gas, I think you need to compare that to the long-term renewable resource that has sustained the region for a long time and the subsistence fishery that has sustained the region as well. Do we want to risk a negative effect on a long-term renewable resource for what may be in the big scheme of things a short-term development? I don't have the answer for you, but I think that's the kind of questions that we need to have and discuss at a forum like this.

MR. STEIN: For the next meeting, it might be useful to have a presentation on what provisions exist now.

BRENT PAINE: I think that's a great idea. My group is relatively new to the world of how to engage in oil and gas development public process. We're pretty good at the public process in terms of the Magnuson-Stevens Act, but this is a new world for us. It would be helpful for my members to really know what that public process is. I've looked at the

Minerals Management Service Web site, emails, and statements about this document out for public review, but it's kind of a morass for me. Plus, I'm too busy doing fisheries stuff to delve into oil and gas; but now we're going to have to because this is looming.

JEFF STEPHAN: That may be something for a follow-up conference where we identify what statutes, regulations, case law, etc., exist. Maybe there's a need for some suggested modifications to legislation.

Q: I'd like to follow up on that question by saying it's not entirely a major oil question whether you have energy production or whether you catch fish.

BRENT PAINE: I agree. I think our largest component of costs is petroleum, in terms of operations. It's pretty high horsepower. Diesel fuel is up to 15 or 20% of our gross value, and that goes into the cost component. Is developing the North Aleutian Basin going to reduce the price of diesel to a fleet of catcher vessels in the Bering Sea?

ERIC OLSON: To follow up on that, there are other areas such as the Arctic National Wildlife Refuge (ANWR) or other areas on the North Slope that might be more amenable to drilling onshore. They have their own issues as well, but some of them may be more amenable to drilling than this area that is home to some of the most productive fishing grounds in the world.

Q: Going back to the memorandum of understanding, I can't help but think of the former Mayor Devens from Valdez who commented that those who are nearest to the development are in a position where they could be grossly impacted by development. I really feel that borough managers, village tribal leaders, fishermen—those who are potentially going to be impacted in that area—should get together and get organized.

Another fact is that oil cleanup equipment did not come into Alaska until we had the huge disaster of the *Exxon Valdez*. When the *Selendang Ayu* hit the shores near Dutch Harbor, they didn't have enough boom to draw in some of that oil. All of the oil spill equipment ended up coming from the North Slope. Local leaders need to come up with a plan that is written down and identified so that a protection plan is already in place when a disaster occurs.

Panel

Perspectives on Energy-Fisheries Coexistence in Norway

Fishery and Aquaculture versus Oil and Gas Activities

Hans Nordgård
Bodø University, High North Center for Business,
Bodø Graduate School of Business, Bodø, Norway

In Norway there has been an intense discussion about the effects that oil and gas drilling, oil and gas production, and oil transport at sea can have on the marine environment. Oil production in Norwegian waters has lasted for 40 years, first in the North Sea in the south and then expanding northward.

Now we have started gas production in the Barents Sea in the north, and there will be oil production as well. A liquefied natural gas plant has been built there, with an investment of $14 billion US.

The petroleum activities of Norway have been important to our economy, so we are now in a situation where we cannot reduce this industry without serious effects on the national economy. With 40 of the 48 Norwegian oil and gas fields now producing less and less, we will have to develop new fields.

During the period of oil activities in the North Sea, great quantities of poisoned water have been poured into the sea, not to mention minor blowouts, without really knowing how it has affected the marine environment.

Scientists cannot give an adequate answer as to why the stocks of North Sea mackerel and herring have declined so rapidly. Something does not fit into the models. Scientists are now working on a total consequence analysis of petroleum activities in the Barents Sea, including the waters of the Lofoten Islands along the northwest coast of northern Norway. This work will be assembled into one report after hearings in 2010, and will be the most important document for making decisions about opening new oil and gas fields in the north.

To the oil companies, the most interesting areas for petroleum activities are from Lofoten to the west coast of Finnmark. But this is also the most biologically vulnerable area. The area is very important to

North Atlantic cod for spawning. They spawn there in the pelagic region, and their eggs and larvae drift in the upper layers of the mixed current of coastal and Atlantic water as they are transported to the Barents sea where they arrive as juveniles. The drifting period from eggs to juveniles is from March to July. Opening up the area for oil production during this period is very risky. A massive blowout could decimate the entire cod stock for one year, approximately 350,000 tons of adult cod.

Trying to gather large amounts of oil from a blowout is impossible, because there is no equipment that can handle such quantities. If the waves are more than 3 meters, and they often are, it is even more difficult. In this area most of the Scando-Atlantic herring stay from December to April and the stock will be about 12 million tons. A lot of other species are in the area, and most of them are also of great economic interest or are an important part of the ecological environment. There are also large colonies of seabirds.

The transport of oil from Murmansk, Russia, to Europe and North America has increased. The traffic now consists of two oil tankers of 100,000 tons daily and it is on the increase. The ships will also increase in size. In a few years there will be more than ten 300,000 ton ships transporting oil through northern Norwegian waters, and there are fishing banks all along the way. That will be the most risky oil activity yet, with the potential to fundamentally harm our marine environment.

The adult fish can escape local pollution but eggs, larvae, and most of the juveniles have no chance. The same situation exists for the aquaculture industry. If oil in the sea reaches the coast, the fish will be damaged and not fit for human consumption. The oil would damage only a small part of the marine farming activity along the entire coastline, but it would be serious enough to affect local companies and communities.

About 90% of Norwegians live on the coast, and almost 100% can reach the coast within one hour. In northern Norway we are especially dependent on marine resources. To illustrate how important the fishery and aquaculture are for the Norwegian economy, the export value of Norwegian fish is about $5.5 billion US. However, the population of Norway is relatively small at 4.5 million people. For the United States, the annual export value of fish is about $17.6 billion.

The debate in Norway about opening the fishing banks outside northwest Norway to oil and gas activities is not so intense at the moment, except among the environmental organizations, because people are waiting for the report to be finished in 2010. After the report is released, I predict that after the final debate in our national assembly the conclusion will be to open for production in one of the three areas, as a start. If that goes well, the next area will follow some years later.

In December 2007 there was an accident in the North Sea where 4,400 tons of oil were pumped into the sea while an oil tanker was loaded. The problem is that the oil tanker crew did not detect it before dawn, because there was no warning system installed to avoid such an incident. In addition, the oil tanker sent an email to the platform which the platform crew did not read before the tanker officer informed them by telephone. Then the oil stream was closed. And most serious, due to weather conditions, it was proved that no equipment was useful to take care of the pollution.

So, stay nervous! Thank you for your attention.

Relationships between Oil & Gas and Fishing Industries in the North Sea UK Sector

James Parker
Shell Oil International Exploration and
Production, Rijswijk, Netherlands

I'm really delighted to speak to you today about some of our experiences in the North Sea, particularly in developing relationships between the oil industry and fisheries.

The North Sea has a very important fishery. To put it in context, in one year Scottish-based vessels landed 380,000 tons of fish to Scottish ports at a value of three-quarters of a billion dollars (Scottish Sea Fisheries Statistics 2006).

Oil and gas development

There are several hydrocarbon development phases, which are shown on the schematic diagram (Fig. 1). During the access phase, we try to get entry to new acreage by obtaining licenses. The access phase is followed by the exploration and appraisal phases, the development phase (engineering design and construction), and then hopefully a long production phase. In the hypothetical situation shown, production could occur from a few years to decades after the appraisal stage, and production can last 25 years or more.

We are continuously investing money until production starts, when we start to make returns on our investment; during decommissioning we then start to spend again. Thus there can be a relatively long period before we actually make returns on our investment. Gaining entry to new areas can extend over many years, and once you start to explore, you could drill a number of unsuccessful wells that would not progress to the development phase. An example was provided in an earlier paper of the somewhat limited successes in St. George Basin.

The early stages of the oil and gas business can sometimes raise expectations about a new industry, but for the reasons given above

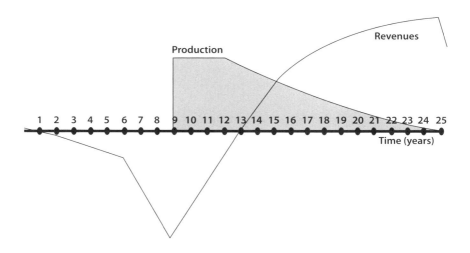

Figure 1. Hydrocarbon development phases. Source: Shell Exploration and Production Company.

these expectations may not actually be realized. Therefore, the industry needs to be cautious at this time about the message we give. Nevertheless, for the North Aleutian Basin. I believe this is exactly the right forum to be communicating in during early development phases, even before the acreage has been licensed.

North Sea perspective

In the North Sea, major oil and gas installations exist off the coast of England, off the Shetland Islands in Scotland, and off the coast of Norway. There are also some oil and gas installations in the Irish Sea and to the west of the Shetlands.

The area covered by the North Sea is about 222,000 square miles. Total seafood landing on average is about 2.5 million tons per year. It has been higher—up to three million tons. These fisheries are under quite a lot of pressure, particularly the cod fishery in recent years. The herring fishery has in the past collapsed as a result of overfishing.

The fisheries can be divided into three groups—the groundfish fishery (500,000 tons); the pelagic fishery, which is primarily herring and mackerel (1 million tons); and the large-scale industrial fishery, fish that go straight to processing plants to become fish meal (1 million tons).

A variety of fishing methods are used from small coastal craft to very large ocean-going vessels. Small, inshore vessels are used for lobster and crab fishing from spring through autumn, for salmon during the summer months, and for longlining for cod in winter. Medium vessels up to 100 feet are most typically seen in the North Sea, but in recent years large 200 foot vessels have come into use.

Fishing and oil industry coexistence

From the following description of North Sea approaches, I hope that you'll be able to appreciate that there are some arrangements that could be valuable when considering the relationship between a future North Aleutian Basin oil and gas industry and fisheries interests.

License conditions

The license conditions issued by the regulator make specific require-ments for fisheries liaison arrangements. Each company must appoint a fisheries liaison officer to liaise between the company and the fishing organizations. The North Sea Industry produced industry guidance on fisheries liaison, which is available at the Web site of Oil and Gas UK, http://www.ukooa.co.uk.

A Fisheries and Offshore Oil Consultative Group, chaired by the government, which brings together representatives of the oil industries and the fishing industries, was also established.

Other license conditions can include special conditions laid down for areas that are particularly sensitive fishing zones. These are built into the conditions that are issued to each operator, depending on the location of the lease the operator is applying for. For new construction activities, operators must consult with fishermen, whose views are taken into account.

There is extensive information on fisheries sensitivities around the North Sea. There are requirements to notify the government before survey operations are undertaken, for example seismic surveys. We consult maps of spawning, nursery, and feeding grounds for all of the major commercial fisheries while planning offshore activities (http://www.cefas.co.uk/media/29947/sensi_maps.pdf).

Compensation

In UK waters, a formal fishermen's compensation fund was established, which is administered by the fishing organizations (http://www.sff.co.uk/ukooa.php). The purpose of the fund is to pay compensation to any fishermen who pick up oil industry debris in their nets. If the debris is attributable to any one operator, that operator will pay. If it is unclear who the operator is, then the compensation fund will pay the compensation.

Design

Subsea structures can be designed with the aim of minimizing the effects of fishing gear interactions. Fig. 2 shows the type of protection

Figure 2. Designs for fishing locations. Source: Shell Exploration and Production Company.

measures that can be built into a subsea well, to protect it from impact by fishing gear. Subsea wellheads are normally designed to take the impact of a substantial unintentional fishing gear interaction.

The design illustrated allows fishermen to reverse the gear back off the wellhead. Tank trials, using a commercial fishing skipper to manipulate the gear, demonstrated the utility of the design.

Fishsafe

Unfortunately, the North Sea has experienced disasters befalling fishing vessels. We had one case in the North Sea where a fishing vessel, the *Westhaven*, caught on a pipeline and was dragged down with the tragic loss of the crew. In the North Sea a system called Fishsafe, available to fishing vessels of any size, is now in place. It works through the GPS on the fishing vessel. The GPS is linked to a comprehensive database of pipeline and subsea equipment locations. It gives an audible and visual warning if the vessel approaches any subsea equipment. It is a good example of a technology developed by the oil industry and fishing industry working together.

Safety zones

For each installation we are required to provide a safety zone of a 500 meter radius around each offshore installation. All vessels have to stay clear of this unless they are actually working for the installation. There are a few exceptions—obviously in an emergency vessels are allowed to enter the safety zone—but the zone normally is closed to fishing and any other maritime activities not associated with the installation.

Discharges

Discharges into the sea are controlled via a permit system. There are internationally agreed-upon discharge limits for oil and water and for certain categories of chemicals. The North Sea is under an international authority framework, and many of our discharges are governed by the Oslo and Paris Commission decisions.

The industry has monitored fish around installations and has demonstrated the absence of significant contamination. Also, government fisheries laboratories have a continuous program of monitoring metals and other potential contaminants in fish from the entire North Sea. North Sea fish are fairly free of contamination arising from the oil and gas industry.

Noise

Noise is also an increasing issue in the North Sea and other waters. Under the International Association of Oil and Gas Producers (OGP), there is a major joint industry project currently investigating the effects of operational noise from our industry on marine organisms.

The issue was raised yesterday about spills and potentially having a bond in place. The UK continental shelf operates the Oil Pollution Offshore Liability (OPOL) agreement, whereby UK offshore operators contribute to a fund to make sure the industry can cover any liabilities from pollution from the offshore industry independent of what that source might be.

Other issues

Other issues that occasionally come up with the industry are the reef effects. Around the platform jackets large accumulations of fish can be present. Following decommissioning, most installations will be entirely removed from the North Sea, but there have been suggestions that these platforms, once decommissioned, could be left in place and developed as a reef fishery. Reef fishing is not normally practiced in the North Sea, although in the southern North Sea there are some gillnetters that fish over wreck sites.

Disturbance to migrations of fish and marine mammals has been raised as a potential issue for the oil industry, but there is little evidence to this effect. Fifteen species of whales and dolphins migrate along a route on the west side of the Shetlands, an area where there are significant offshore operations.

I located an early document called *Questions and Answers about Fish and Offshore Oil Development*, by Keith G. Hay (1984, American Petroleum Institute publication 875-5932, Washington, D.C., 69 pp.). This booklet provides answers to a variety of questions that fishermen may have about our industry, such as what are the impacts of oil spills, what are drilling muds and cuttings, are drilling muds and cuttings a threat to fish life, etc. About 60 questions are answered, pertinent to today's topic. Participants might want to revisit this book.

Conclusions

My concluding remark is that fishing and oil and gas industries need to keep each other well informed, of what our business activities are, and we need to consult with each other and resolve any problems that arise between our industries.

The University of Alaska Fairbanks has provided an excellent forum for this early discussion on the Aleutian Basin.

Perspectives on Energy-Fisheries Coexistence in Norway: Audience Questions and Answers

DAVE HARBOUR: I retired as Commissioner on the Regulatory Commission of Alaska a couple of weeks ago. I think this activity leads to dispassionate adjudication and I appreciate the forum. Is the fisheries offshore consultation group in the United Kingdom a rough equivalent of the One Ocean concept that's employed in Canada?

JAMES PARKER: Yes, it's a very similar type of organization. In a sense, it's independently adjudicated by the government departments. There are representatives from the fishery industry, government, and the oil and gas industry. There are representatives of the offshore operators association and of the Scottish fishermen's federation, and I think the National Federation of Fishing Organization. I'm not sure what the arrangements are in Norway. I'm sure you will have similar arrangements and the Norwegians may want to comment on that.

GORDON SLADE: Just to mention, I spoke yesterday about One Ocean. I want to clarify that the government is not involved in One Ocean. One Ocean is composed of the fishing industry and the oil and gas industry. Governments only sit on the board as ex officio members. The Coast Guard and the Department of Fisheries and Oceans and the oil regulator sit on the board in an ex officio capacity.

Q: How are the herring stocks doing in Norway? What about wild salmon stocks?

HANS NORDGÅRD: We are fishing salmon stocks, but not in great quantities. They are strictly regulated. The herring stock has come back and it's growing fast and the stock is in very good condition.

Q: I have heard reports from Norway that seismic vessels are chasing salmon. They were being referred to as cowboys of the seas or something of that nature. Can you give us some idea of what's happening to that?

HANS NORDGÅRD: Yes, there are at least two questions about seismic activities. One question is, Who should have the place on the sea surface, the fishermen or the seismic ships? The seismic itself harms the fish for a time when the seismic is shot. There have been some problems where seismic ships have done their work when the fishermen are out fishing at the same areas.

PER EIDSVIK: I can support Hans and say that we do know that it's not necessary for so many companies to operate at the same time. We also think that operations must be better coordinated. Lost income has to be compensated, and that includes industry onshore. We also need more technology for seismic.

BEN GREEN: I'm with the Alaska Department of Natural Resources. Thank you very much for your presentations. They're very informative and useful. I'm hoping that you can speak about discharges, and I'm referring not only to the cuttings and the muds from drilling, but also produced water and what we call gray water and black water.

I am not familiar with the process of regulating discharges in Norway. I've heard there is a no discharge policy for exploration, development, and production and then I've also heard that "no discharges" actually doesn't mean no discharges. Could you please clarify?

PER EIDSVIK: Yes, we have taken many years to reach this goal of no discharge, especially of produced water. That's very important for us. I think the next goal is to reduce carbon emissions to zero.

JAMES PARKER: I'll give a brief answer from the UK sector. The entire area almost to Norway is actually covered by the international convention, called the Oslo and Paris Convention. That convention provides the framework regulation of all discharges from the offshore industry. Produced water is regulated to those international standards. All of the member states must agree to the oil and water discharge conditions. On an annual basis, all countries report discharges from their offshore installations. It is possible in some areas to re-inject produced water, but it's not possible everywhere, so some installations can do it, some can't. Again, you really need to go back to the science of this, because over many years we carried out experiments on produced water and the toxicity of produced water.

Panel

Oil & Gas Impact

The Physical Toxicity Side of Oil and Gas: Are Seismic Surveys an Important Risk Factor for Fish and Shellfish?

Jerry Payne
Department of Fisheries and Oceans, St. Johns, Newfoundland, Canada

I have been involved in ecotoxicology for some time and only recently got into the seismic end of things. Most of my interest in relation to oil and gas activities has been more or less on the chemical toxicity side, investigating the potential effects of discharges, namely drilling muds and produced waters as well as hydrocarbons in general. The emphasis has primarily been placed on chronic toxicity studies with fish and shellfish.

Introduction

Oil development is presently taking place on the Grand Banks of Newfoundland, traditionally one of the world's richest fishing grounds. Oil companies currently working different fields in the offshore include Exxon-Mobil, Husky, and Petro Canada. Similar to discussions taking place at this workshop, there were some initial concerns in Newfoundland about the coexistence of the fishing and oil industries.

One of the key observations of note for the Grand Banks area is that all developers have in place quite good environmental effects monitoring (EEM) programs. Their programs include use of early warning systems (e.g., biochemical and pathological indicators) for detecting effects on fish and shellfish, as well as fish and shellfish tainting—the latter being of major importance for assessing product quality and thus market acceptability. Also included are more commonly used monitoring indices such as assessment of benthic community structure and sediment toxicity.

The fishery on the Grand Banks was historically prosecuted by small boats, but large trawlers also became a major component of fishing efforts in later years. Snow crab is presently one of the main fisheries that has replaced cod (and flounder), which suffered a major decline due to overfishing (and probably changing oceanographic conditions). At one time, up to 800,000 tons of cod were landed per year from the Grand Banks and adjacent waters. By contrast, one of our research trawlers can now drag for 20 minutes without striking a single fish. There is still some fishing for cod in coastal bays in Newfoundland, but the offshore fishery is under moratorium.

Seismic impacts on fisheries

The basic principle of seismic testing with airguns is that, since rock, oil, etc., have different densities, signatures reflecting sound will be somewhat different for each. Seismic survey ships commonly deploy several heavy airguns with hydrophone streamers extending astern for several kilometers.

Although considerable attention has been given to the potential effects of seismic on the behavior of marine mammals, as well as the possibility for producing adverse physiological effects such as on hearing, lesser attention has been given to potential effects on fish and shellfish.

There is evidence that some fish species may undergo temporary displacement during a seismic survey. Fish larvae and eggs may also suffer immediate mortality within a few meters of a heavy sound source. However, it is sublethal effects that are most difficult to deal with, and serious physiological and anatomical damage may be occurring in adult fish and shellfish at depth in the water column.

We have carried out a number of preliminary seismic trials in the laboratory with several species including cunners, cod, crab, lobster, shrimp, smelt, jellyfish, and capelin. Various numbers of airgun shots have been employed (25, 50, etc.) with measured sound pressure levels in the 202 dB peak-to-peak range. No mortalities were observed, but we have obtained evidence from sublethal effects studies on lobster and cod that the issue of potential for seismic to produce sublethal effects in marine organisms should be given more attention. Similar cautionary statements have been made by Robert McCauley (Australia) and Arthur Popper (USA) who provided evidence a few years ago for ear damage in fish upon exposure to seismic.

Lobster

Lobster is one of the most commercially important species in Atlantic Canada. We exposed lobster to a "low" level of sound in the laboratory and a "high" level in the field.

Exposure of lobster to low (202 dB peak-to-peak) and high (227 dB peak-to-peak) sound levels had no effects on delayed mortality up to 8 months post-exposure, mechano-balancing systems (as demonstrated by lack of effects on righting ability), or loss of appendages. However, sublethal effects were observed with respect to feeding and serum biochemistry (selected enzymes, calcium, and protein) with statistically significant effects sometimes being retained weeks to months after low-level exposures. Feeding was generally characterized by an increase in food consumption, which is of interest since food intake has been reported to increase in humans (as well as in mammalian models) subjected to brain trauma. A histochemical change (elevated deposits of carbohydrate) was also noted in the hepatopancreas of animals exposed four months previously.

Studies such as the one briefly described with lobster can be informative since it is known that population level effects short of major or catastrophic impacts would be very difficult to detect through stock assessment studies in the open ocean.

A study carried out by Australian workers on rock lobster populations is mentioned in this regard. This study noted no effect on lobster populations in areas where seismic surveys had been carried out, but cautioned that seismic-induced reductions in the 50% range would be required before being amenable to statistical resolution.

Cod

Likewise, in preliminary studies conducted on Atlantic cod, no mortalities were observed, but sublethal and possible debilitating effects were found. As for lobster, one of the most interesting of these effects was altered feeding characterized by an increase in food consumption for up to a month after exposure.

One of the other interesting observations was the tendency for exposed cod to remain near the bottom of the tank for about two weeks. Fish catches have been reported on occasion to increase in conjunction with seismic surveys, and it has been suggested that fish may "cluster" and swim closer to the bottom, facilitating greater catch rates. Our tank observations with cod lend support to such a hypothesis for fish movement.

We are presently employing genomic tools to extend the range of our sublethal effects research. Some preliminary studies have been carried out with juvenile cod and we have obtained evidence for both up and down regulation of genes in the brains of fish exposed to seismic sounds. Might change in neural gene regulation be linked to the observations on feeding?

Monkfish

We are also now involved in a study with the fishermen's union in Newfoundland (Fish Food and Allied Workers) on the potential effects of seismic on monkfish eggs. Monkfish are unique in that they release their eggs in large gelatinous veils that may float for weeks on or near the ocean surface. Fishermen were keen for such a study since they fish monkfish in an area south of Newfoundland, the Laurentian Sub-Basin, which is also an area of interest for oil exploration.

Snow crab

A preliminary opportunistic study carried out by a consulting company in Newfoundland noted retarded development of detached snow crab eggs exposed to an high number of airgun shots. We believe that one of the priority areas for further research would be an assessment of the potential for seismic to affect molting and internal egg development in commercially important species such as snow crab and lobsters. Such research would be of value for fisheries interests in Alaska as well as Eastern Canada.

Future general directions

The initial studies we have carried out on sublethal effects were meant to be exploratory in nature, and caution is warranted about overinterpretation. However, the results do reinforce a need for development of at least a rough appreciation of "dose-response" relationships for the effects of seismic on representative marine organisms. Having said this, it is recognized that even a few experiments carried out in the field along the lines of an actual seismic survey and employing different energy levels (in relation to water depth) would generally be considered to be prohibitively expensive (certainly in the millions of dollars range). However, biological impact studies can reasonably be addressed in a cost effective manner through use of large aquaria and small-scale field exposures, with animals being subsequently retained in the laboratory for periodic analysis and observation.

Tank experiments also provide a practical means for obtaining information on cumulative or chronic effects, for which there is presently a complete knowledge gap. Such experiments would simulate conditions whereby animals would be subjected to relatively high noise levels for extended periods, mimicking conditions in the field where surveys may extend for three weeks or more. Chronic exposures wrought by seismic surveys might for instance negatively affect neurohormonal systems leading to adverse effects such as on reproduction. Thus some attention should be given to the potential for chronic as well as "acute" effects of seismic exposure.

Conclusions

It is premature at this time to adopt sound pressure guidelines for fish and shellfish without some knowledge of the potential size of injury zones (i.e., injury/energy relationships) during seismic surveys.

Injury zones may not exist to any major extent, but inferences cannot be made with any degree of confidence in the absence of empirical data. Furthermore, representative studies are needed on fish and shellfish if only for assurance.

Field studies employing seismic survey ships would be both logistically difficult and prohibitively expensive, but important range finding data can be obtained in a very cost effective manner through laboratory and small-scale field experiments.

Further viewpoint is provided in the following publications:

Payne, J.F., C.A. Andrews, L.L. Fancey, A.L. Cook, and J.R. Christian. 2008. Pilot study on the effects of seismic airgun noise on lobster (*Homarus americanus*). Canadian Technical Report of Fisheries and Aquatic Science 2712, 46 pp.

Payne, J.F., C.A. Andrews, L.L. Fancey, D. White, and J.R. Christian. 2008. Potential effects of seismic energy on fish and shellfish: An update since 2003. Canadian Science Advisory Secretariat, Research Document number 60.

National Pollutant Discharge Elimination System (NPDES) Permit Process

Cindi Godsey, Environmental Engineer
EPA Alaska Operations, Anchorage, Alaska

The NPDES (National Pollutant Discharge Elimination System) is the permitting process authorized under Section 402 of the U.S. Clean Water Act, and the Environmental Protection Agency (EPA) issues the permits for these discharges in Alaska at the present time. The permits are meant to control the discharge of pollutants from point sources into waters of the United States. Permits have to be consistent with the Coastal Zone Management Act, which is administered by the State of Alaska. In state waters the permits must be certified by the Alaska Department of Environmental Conservation (ADEC), as complying with state water quality standards, CWA §401.

Outer continental shelf (OCS) waters are federal waters greater than three miles offshore or outside the baseline. The State of Alaska does not certify NPDES permits for this area, nor does it certify the portions of a broader permit that covers this area plus additional areas. The state does certify the portion that applies to state waters. In OCS waters, EPA rather than ADEC issues air permits

Currently EPA drafts permits, issues permits, conducts compliance inspections and tracks compliance, and takes enforcement action where necessary. ADEC is in the process of preparing an application to take over the permitting program for those areas where the state can do so. That application is due into EPA sometime in the spring.

Permit process for oil and gas exploration

For oil and gas exploration, regulation 122.28(c) in 40 CFR says that the EPA shall issue general permits. Also in the regulation is the requirement that EPA draft a permit, and be in the process of issuing a permit when Minerals Management Service (MMS) is at the draft environmental

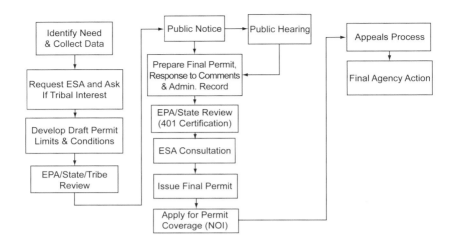

Figure 1. General EPA permitting process.

impact statement (EIS) stage. In addition, a schedule must be included for the final issuance of the permit, which should be six months after the date of the request or coincide with the date of the final notice of sale projected by MMS—sometimes it does and more often it doesn't.

In the general permitting process (Fig. 1), EPA first identifies that a general permit is necessary. For example, an MMS lease sale would be the impetus in OCS waters. EPA is required to deal with the federal service agencies for endangered species and essential fish habitat, and has to ask if the tribes in the area would like to participate in tribal consultation.

Next EPA develops a draft permit that will contain the limits and conditions, and will have EPA's date and tribal review of the pre-draft. Also, at this time if the state needs to certify, they'll provide EPA with a draft certification to be included in the public notice.

Sometimes EPA has a public hearing, but not always. It is not a requirement. If there is interest in the process EPA can schedule one with public notice. If a public hearing is not scheduled, people can request that one be held.

After receiving comments EPA prepares the final permit and the response to comments, as well as the administrative record. The state will do the final 401 certification, and then EPA wraps up any Endangered Species Act consultation that is needed and issues the final permit.

When the permit is issued, there is a 30 day time frame before the permit is effective. The appeal process for the permit is handled in the Ninth Circuit court, and the appeal period is 120 days after issuance. Therefore, the permit goes into effect before the appeal process is over, and the permit actually stays in effect unless the court says it isn't in effect. If there is an appeal, then EPA will work either through mediation or reissuance of the permit and come to a final agency action.

Discharges

The exploration permit for the Chukchi and Beaufort seas contains limits, requirements, and conditions for 14 different types of discharges. When EPA considers a permit for the North Aleutian Basin to go with MMS's lease sale, these are likely the same types of discharges that you'll see covered in the act.

Discharges covered by Chukchi and Beaufort seas permit

- Drilling fluids and drilling cuttings

- Deck drainage

- Sanitary wastes

- Domestic wastes

- Desalination unit wastes

- Blowout preventer fluid

- Boiler blowdown

- Fire control system test water

- Non-contact cooling water

- Uncontaminated ballast water

- Bilge water

- Excess cement slurry

- Mud, cuttings, cement at seafloor

- Test fluids

Evaluation of impacts

40 CFR 125, Subpart M, is the section of the regulations that contains the requirements for ocean discharge criteria, to evaluate the impacts that a permitted activity may have on the environment. It requires that EPA make a determination that a discharge or, in the consideration of

a general permit, the possibility of multiple discharges, won't cause unreasonable degradation of the marine environment. And in conjunction with the draft permit, EPA publishes an ocean discharge criteria evaluation (ODCE) for this purpose. An ODCE is actually required by regulation for any discharge outside the baseline—generally a designated geographic line that can cross estuaries and bays and inlets and the like. Inside the baseline it's not a requirement.

ODCE: *Unreasonable degradation*

- Significant adverse changes in ecosystem diversity, productivity, and stability of the biological community within the area of discharge and surrounding biological communities.

- Threat to human health through direct exposure to pollutants or through consumption of exposed aquatic organisms.

- Loss of aesthetic, recreational, scientific, or economic values, which are unreasonable in relation to the benefit derived from the discharge.

Unreasonable degradation determination criteria

1. The quantities, composition, and potential for bioaccumulation or persistence of the pollutants to be discharged.

2. The potential transport of such pollutants by biological, physical, or chemical processes.

3. The composition and vulnerability of the biological communities that may be exposed to such pollutants, including the presence of unique species or communities of species, the presence of species identified as endangered or threatened pursuant to the Endangered Species Act (ESA), or the presence of those species critical to the structure or function of the ecosystem, such as those important for the food chain.

4. The importance of the receiving water area to the surrounding biological community, including the presence of spawning sites, nursery/forage areas, migratory pathways, or areas necessary for other functions or critical stages in the life cycle of an organism.

5. The existence of special aquatic sites including, but not limited to, marine sanctuaries and refuges, parks, national and historic monuments, national seashores, wilderness areas, and coral reefs.

6. The potential impacts on human health through direct and indirect pathways.

7. Existing or potential recreational and commercial fishing, including finfish and shellfish.

8. Any applicable requirements of an approved Coastal Zone Management Plan.

9. Such other factors relating to the effects of the discharge as may be appropriate.

10. Marine water quality criteria developed pursuant to Section 304(a) (1).

Contact information

Cindi Godsey
Environmental Protection Agency
222 W. 7th Avenue, Box 19
Anchorage, AK 99577
(907) 271-6561

Mercury in Drilling Fluids

Richard Prentki
Minerals Management Service, Alaska OCS Region, Anchorage, Alaska

Mary C. Boatman
*Minerals Management Service, Environmental
Sciences Branch, Herndon, Virginia*

Mercury in drilling fluids became an issue with offshore oil and gas drilling because of concerns raised in a series of articles in the *Mobile Register* in late 2001-2002, regarding the results of a Minerals Management Service (MMS) study, the Gulf of Mexico Offshore Operations Monitoring Experiment (GOOMEX). Surface sediment samples were collected from five platforms in the Gulf of Mexico during the GOOMEX study and analyzed for total mercury. While this study was reported in 1995, the 2001-2002 newspaper articles sparked interest in the potential for drilling discharges to be contributing to the elevated levels of mercury. As part of GOOMEX, samples were collected from near the platform and far from the platform. Total mercury ranged from "not detected" to 3.5 parts per million. The highest values were from near a single platform where discharges are shunted to within ten meters of the bottom, to limit their dispersion. Tissue samples including shrimp, crabs, fish livers, and fish stomach contents were also collected as part of the project and analyzed for total mercury. Statistical comparison of the results indicated that the samples did not differ significantly between near field and far field.

Mercury occurs in the environment in three basic forms: elemental mercury, inorganic mercury, and organic mercury. Elemental mercury is the silver liquid you see in a glass thermometer. It is also present in the air as a gas. Inorganic mercury is a metal cation. It can be dissolved in water or bound to an anion in a mineral, commonly with sulfur as in the mineral cinnabar. Other mercury forms can be converted to organic mercury (methylmercury) primarily by a few species of bacteria. This requires a mildly reducing environment. Methylmercury is the form most easily taken up by biota and is considered the most toxic form.

Mercury is the only metal contaminant that commonly biomagnifies up the food chain. That is, the predator ends up with a higher body concentration of mercury than was in its food. This biomagnification increases the risk of mercury poisoning. In humans, the effects include deterioration of the nervous system; impaired hearing, speech, and vision; involuntary muscle movements, etc.

Major past and present industrial uses of mercury include gold mining, chlor-alkali plants, paper plants, agriculture, latex paints, dental amalgam, and household products. Most of these uses have decreased or been banned since about 1990. Mercury amalgamation for gold recovery on gold dredges at Nome, Alaska, was stopped by the Environmental Protection Agency in 1987.

Mercury is a global pollutant, with most mercury entering the environment through the air. Roughly 85% of U.S. mercury emissions in 1994-1995 came from coal and other combustion (municipal and medical incinerators, etc.) sources. At least one consumption advisory regarding unsafe mercury levels in fish have been issued in 35 of the 50 states. Alaska was added to this list on February 26, 2008, with an advisory on lake trout in the Noatak National Preserve on the Seward Peninsula.

A U.S. Geological Survey study of ice cores from the Fremont Glacier in Wyoming found a 20-fold increase in mercury deposition over the last 100 years. Better recent environmental management of mercury reduced this increase to only 10-fold over baseline in the last decade. Dated sediment cores from an MMS study of lower Cook Inlet and Shelikof Strait, Alaska, downcurrent from offshore oil and gas development in Cook Inlet, do not show a similar increase in mercury deposition over baseline back to at least 1920. Thus this part of Alaska, at the same latitude as the North Aleutian Basin, may be better off than the Lower 48.

Mercury in drilling fluids is present in barite used as a weighting agent. Barite makes up about 40% of the drilling fluid by weight. Mercury concentrations in barite are limited by EPA regulations to less than 1 part per million (ppm). One summary study of the Gulf of Mexico (with a few thousand oil and gas platforms) estimated that about 0.3% of mercury in the gulf was from oil industry discharges. A second study of methylmercury in sediment adjacent to offshore drilling sites in the Gulf of Mexico concluded that 99.9% of methylmercury was generated from natural mercury. A third study found that mercury in barite was insoluble in seawater, digestive-strength acid, and in anoxic seawater. Mineralogical tests indicated the mercury was associated with insoluble sulfide minerals.

The MMS in Alaska has funded several studies that examined mercury issues on the Alaska Outer Continental Shelf (OCS). A workshop (MMS 90-0059), field sampling (MMS 90-0010), and mercury in hair study (MMS 91-0065) were conducted in preparation for an OCS gold sale off of Nome. The Sediment Quality in Depositional Areas of Shelikof Strait and Outermost Cook Inlet study (MMS 2000-024) was conducted to look for contaminants, including mercury, downcurrent from the Cook Inlet offshore oil industry. The Arctic Nearshore Impact Monitoring in Development Area (ANIMIDA) (MMS 2001-104, MMS 2005-051) and continuation of ANIMIDA (cANIMIDA, MMS 2005-036, p. 33), looked for contaminants, including mercury, in the area of oil development offshore of Prudhoe Bay. Separate Coastal Marine Institute, University of Alaska Fairbanks studies (MMS 2001-061, MMS 2003-057, MMS 2005-041) have also looked for anthropogenic contaminants, including mercury, in the nearshore Beaufort Sea from Barrow almost to Canada. To date, levels of mercury found in Alaska sediments appear to be at background levels.

Thus in both the Gulf of Mexico and Alaska marine waters, there is no evidence that oil and gas activities contribute measurably to environmental mercury levels, including in biota such as fish.

Oil & Gas Impact: Audience Questions and Answers

Q: When they were dredging off the coast of Nome they found mercury in some of the walruses and sea lions, as I recall in the liver.

RICHARD PRENTKI: I don't recall what the concentrations of mercury were in the marine mammals. Some of the marine mammals accumulate mercury in organs and it is stored as organic mercury. I don't think that is attributed to gold mining. The problem they had with the water sample data was that they discovered they were contaminating their samples in the lab by doing gold amalgamation in the same place they put the water samples. When we had somebody else do water analyses, the mercury concentration numbers were very low.

Q: Is the current rule that just 1% mercury is allowed?

RICHARD PRENTKI: One part per million.

Q: Who monitors that?

RICHARD PRENTKI: Analyses are sent to the Environmental Protection Agency (EPA). When the EPA did our Gulf of Mexico studies, they looked at the concentration of mercury in the drilling muds. The average amount they found was about a half a part per million. They were well below that on average.

Q: So the company sends in their samples?

CINDI GODSEY: The analysis for drilling fluids and drill cuttings is a requirement of the exploration permits that the EPA has now. It's been a while since I've looked at one of these permits, but I believe that mercury in the muds and cuttings is one of the tests that they have to evaluate for. And yes, the National Pollutant Discharge Elimination System (NPDES) is a self-monitoring program.

Q: I've worked for Shell and I just wanted to clarify that drilling muds are tested by an independent lab. Those tests would show under the one part per million limit. Typically it comes in at a range between 0.2 and 0.9 parts per million. I think what Dick said is accurate—if you look an average it's about a half a part per million.

Q: You might also have checked out some of the previous studies in Alaska and three or four in the Beaufort Sea in the late 1970s and early 1980s. In none of those studies did they find any amount of mercury above one part per million. Also, it's well documented in Canadian literature from the 1970s that mercury levels accumulate in marine mammals.

Q: My first question is for Dick. Who funded your studies?

RICHARD PRENTKI: Most of our studies are funded by the Minerals Management Service (MMS). There might have been co-funding on some of the Gulf of Mexico studies, but the Alaska ones are funded by MMS.

Q: I'm curious if the seismic studies that were done around Newfoundland looked at fish stocks. It was noted that after seismic tests around Australia and on the East Coast, a number of whales beached themselves. Were there any studies done on fish with air bladders and the effects of seismic?

JERRY PAYNE: No, not really. I'm familiar with the studies on hearing carried out in Australia. We would like to see further studies in this area. You wouldn't expect decimation, but could have serious ablation of ear cell cilia.

One of the effects we investigated in lobster was loss of equilibrium through putative injury to the statocyst, a mechano-balancing organ. There are still questions to me in terms of sublethal effects, that need to be studied more intensely. There is some information on sonar in terms of marine mammals.

Q: I have just a couple of follow-ups. It's really important for folks to understand that study results are very dependent upon the exact location and on the species. And I am curious if you've looked at stress hormones with respect to noise on fish and other critters?

JERRY PAYNE: We've looked at some hormones. We know from lab experience that when fish are disturbed cortisol levels increase. If fish are chronically disturbed, cortisol levels will go up over a period of weeks and this has, at least, been associated with deformed larvae in cod. No studies of this nature have been carried out with seismic but it is one of the reasons for suggesting some attention be given to chronic exposures of fish to seismic sounds.

Panel

North Aleutian Basin Potentially Impacted Communities—Opportunities and Concerns

Welcome to the City of Unalaska

Shirley Marquardt, Mayor
City of Unalaska, Alaska

Thank you for the opportunity to participate in this ongoing discussion. It seems like it's early to be talking about planning and opportunities, but when I look at the leasing process and how many years and different steps it is going to take along the way, we are probably right on time. I think it's critical that agencies, stakeholder communities, and interested individuals are involved in this every step of the way.

The Port of Dutch Harbor and the City of Unalaska are truly geographically blessed. We're the only deepwater, ice-free port on the great circle route between the U.S. West Coast and East Asia. Thanks to the critical basic infrastructure left by the military when they pulled out in the late 1940s, the city had a good base for the reconstruction of a community that could support significant growth in the private and public sector. The building effort over the last 20 years has created a support system for fishing interests that almost 70 years later has made it the number-one fishing port in the United States—number one in landings, number two in value, for 17 years running.

Unalaska is a fascinating mix of old and new, past and future. We have large-scale industrial processing, a diverse and healthy fishing industry, successful small businesses, multi-unit housing, and single-family homes. We're extremely diverse in our cultures, in our interests, and in what we do for a living. Our 4,000 full-time citizens have a pretty good life in Unalaska because of our healthy economy and quality of life services and facilities.

On the industrial side of Unalaska is the UniSea Complex. They are the largest of the three processors on the island, and have over 1,000 employees processing pollock, cod, and crab year-round. Our 3,900 foot paved runway is new in the last 20 years, as is the airport terminal, to keep up with an average of more than 30,000 landings and take-offs a year. When I first arrived in Unalaska in 1980, it was still a very small town. About 400 people lived there, with very limited public infrastructure and community programs. Then came the groundfish industry, and millions of dollars in infrastructure projects were built to support the fishing industry, which provided us with job opportunities and fish tax revenues that literally built the community from the bottom up.

Our port welcomes most of the Bering Sea fleet almost 12 months out of the year and we support them year-round with our docks, roads, water system, landfill, transportation companies, businesses, taxis, restaurants, and supply stores. And they support us with fish tax dollars, primarily paid directly to the state, with a portion shared to the City of Unalaska. Approximately $8 to $10 million a year comes directly back to Unalaska as revenue from fish taxes, and we generally put it directly into the infrastructure that's needed to support the industry. The City of Unalaska has its own 3% raw fish tax, 3% sales tax, and 11.78 mil property tax—the bulk of that property tax paid by the shore plants in our area.

Something is always going on in Unalaska. We have major fisheries that are opening and closing nearly year-round. A vessel may change from pot gear to trawl, or a company might go after the same species with a different vessel. Because of the conservative, science-based fisheries policy decisions made by the North Pacific Fishery Management Council we are able to project revenues 3 to 5 years in advance and plan our expenditures accordingly.

We have a new project coming to town. American Seafoods decided that in order to better compete in the worldwide market against Russian and Chinese fish products, they need a cold storage unit so they can ship out entire pollock orders to Asia and Europe. It's a 35,000 square foot, two-story, state-of-the-art cold storage unit, plus 1,000 feet of filled dock space, which we really need in our community. The dock part of the project is three-quarters of the way finished. By the time the project is open for business, they will have invested over $100 million dollars in our community. It will benefit the entire region, not just the pollock fishery and Unalaska.

Unalaska is the home of the westernmost container terminals in the state, and is one of the most productive ports for transshipment of cargo in Alaska. Products are not only shipped domestically to and from this regional hub, they are also shipped to such foreign markets as South Korea, Japan, Norway, China, Spain, Israel, Denmark, the United Kingdom, and Malaysia. According to the U.S. Army Corps of Engineers, over one million short tons of cargo passed through Unalaska in 2007, and nearly 3 million metric tons were shipped from Unalaska to Asia and Europe.

When you're doing your long-range planning you have to take into consideration that at some point your revenues will stop coming in real high, and when the boom ends, you better not have created an operating budget that requires an endless boom to pay for it. Unfortunately, that's close to what Unalaska has done. Our revenues rise at about 1% a year, but our operation costs to keep up with the infrastructure needs and public employees rises at almost 7% per year.

Capital projects in the next 5-10 years for the City of Unalaska would cost over $250 million if all on the capital planning list were to be funded, and more if we add a geothermal project to our list. As most people know, if they're part of a municipality, finding funding for capital projects is a challenge with both state and federal money. But we need all these improvements in order to keep our industry healthy and keep our community secure. It is the price that comes with a new and booming industry.

City of Unalaska capital projects:

- Unalaska Marine Center position III replacement

- Carl Moses small boat harbor

- Power house expansion

- Wastewater treatment plant

- Road paving

- South channel bridge

- Landfill

- Airport runway expansion

The City of Unalaska Makushin Geothermal Project would involve a geothermal resource on a bench about 1,200 feet up on Makushin, an active volcano. There have been test drills since 1982. However, the challenges of constructing on that bench and actually operating probably take this project out of the realm of reality.

A new bridge was built in town by the state. During the five years it was under construction, it went from an $8 million project to a $29 million project. We're in the process of designing a new landfill for the next 40 years. Our landfill filled up eight years ahead of schedule simply because of the strength of the fisheries participants that our community supports.

Although Unalaska enjoys a strong economy due to the high volume of cargo shipments through its ports, it is also faced with many challenges as a result of our proximity to the great circle route. Dutch Harbor is the key potential port of refuge (PPR) for distressed/disabled vessels in the Aleutian chain, and in 2006 the badly disabled and listing M/V *Cougar Ace* was brought right into our city waters, bringing ballast water contamination and fuel spill risks. Thankfully, she was righted without any problem; it took about a week and half to very slowly bring her up, and off she sailed. But we weren't so lucky other times. There have been many oil spills from fishing vessels and freighters in the Aleutians. And we had the M/V *Selendang Ayu* and M/V *Kuroshima* disasters. The *Selendang Ayu* broke in two and six lives were lost. They spilled around 350,000 gallons of fuel, which took two years to clean up. The cost was well over $100 million and it closed a local bairdi and Tanner crab fishery for two winters. The entire Aleutian chain, including Unalaska Island, is a National Marine Wildlife Refuge, so there are always environmental challenges that go along with having a great economy.

On the positive side, our clinic was primarily paid for by fisheries money—the shore plants and the fishing companies and boats. They contributed the money and helped build the clinic more than 20 years ago, and they continue to support it. The Grand Aleutian Hotel was very strongly supported by fishery dollars and it also gives the community a nice place to go for weddings, parties, receptions, and get-togethers.

Our Museum of the Aleutians would not have been built without fisheries money. Our library with its computer access is very heavily used by fishermen and visitors to the community, as well as our school kids. Fisheries money has paid for community parks, a beautiful and responsive Parks and Recreation Center, a pool, road paving, and school operating budgets.

As Unalaskans, we love our island and we will fiercely protect it. We've learned to deal with industry and we do understand that there is a way for responsible business and environmental standards to move forward together. The fishing industry has been very responsive to our concerns, and the transportation sector knows that nobody wants to see spilled oil again in Unalaska on our beaches and on the rocks.

Economic growth has been phenomenal for our community. It has raised the quality of life to a point where people choose to move here— they want to live in Unalaska. Our young people go off to school, and after they finish they come back; they want to stay.

Our greatest concern about potential oil and gas exploration in the Aleutian basin at this point is how we are going to plan years in advance for something that may or may not happen. It's a risk, but if we're going to get wheels turning for projects for roads, for dock improvements to help support an industry that may be coming in our direction, we've got to start now. It's going to be a real challenge, but we're looking forward to it and we're also looking forward to working with our neighbors along the chain as we go forward. So, thank you very much.

Opportunities versus Risk for Our Communities

Justine Gundersen
Nelson Lagoon Village, Alaska

Our communities have discussed the concerns and opportunities with the advent of potential oil and gas development. Our concern is universal: an oil spill, which would devastate our sea life, our commercial fishing, and our migratory bird population. This also has been the resounding concern at this conference. While the oil spill risk exists, and there is always risk with any development, I believe we have to go through the process, we have to continue the dialogue as this develops, such as having more conferences like this one.

Aleutians East Borough leaders have sat down with the oil industry from the inception telling them what their concerns are, what the expectations are for the whole area. We have our mitigation measures established; we are not letting anything escape our attention. The opportunities for the region include jobs for our young people, revenue sharing for all of the regions, roads, improved transportation, and individuals developing their own support business. Our young people are moving away because they do not want to commercial fish. Our communities are getting smaller because we can no longer rely on commercial fishing to support us. Our fuel prices are high and we are not able to sustain ourselves through winter. We need another industry to give this region a future.

Having said that, we will proceed with looking and learning and discussing. The people of the coastal communities are natural environmentalists; they guard their lifestyle, but understand change. The risk will be there; we are learning.

North Aleutian Basin Energy Fisheries: Dillingham Opportunities and Concerns

Tim Sands
Dillingham City Council, Dillingham, Alaska

Dillingham is a relatively small community—only 2,400 people or so—but we do it all on our own. We're a first class city; we're responsible for our own school district and all our own taxes, etc. There are a lot of cities bigger than Dillingham that aren't first class cities.

We are the economic, transportation, and public services hub for western Bristol Bay, and we are a regional center for government and services. We have a hospital, and regional centers for the University of Alaska Fairbanks Bristol Bay Campus, Bristol Bay Housing Authority, Alaska Department of Fish and Game, U.S. Fish and Wildlife Service, etc., in Dillingham.

Commercial fishing obviously is our main industry, and fish processing, cold storage, and support of the fishing industry are also primary activities. I am the manager for the west side of Bristol Bay commercial fishery. Salmon and herring are a big part of our industry, but we don't have a lot of fish taxes because much of the processing is done offshore on floaters. Also, many of the residents, including myself, subsist on fish and wildlife and that's a very big part of the economy. Prices are high for food and everything else in Dillingham.

Dillingham is a traditionally Yupik Eskimo village. There is some Russian influence and, of course, we're diversifying over time. In addition to commercial fishing, there is sportfishing. We are a jumping off point to several of the refuges in the area. The Tikchik State Park is the largest state park in the United States and the Nushagak River has one of the best king salmon runs in the world.

Dillingham position on oil and gas development

In 2003 the Dillingham City Council passed a resolution supporting onshore oil and gas development, but there's a lot of trepidation about offshore development. The issues are added economic benefit versus the risk to our current economy of subsistence and commercial fishing. The habitat is very sensitive.

One of the knocks on Dillingham has been that Dillingham is opposed to everything. Pebble Mine development is a big issue in Dillingham right now, and the City Council is opposed to that. But there are many things that we're in favor of: commercial salmon fishing, enhanced salmon quality, competing in the global market, commercial recreation, small business development—we salute the entrepreneur and structure, local codes and taxes, preservation of culture and current quality of life, and onshore oil/gas development. In addition we say yes to partnerships (city/tribe, school/city, etc.); small-scale mineral resource development (gravel, etc.); alternative energy and developing it responsibly; "paying our own way" with a 13 mil property tax, 6% sales tax, and 10% bed/alcohol tax; and volunteerism/civic responsibility.

We do want to be part of the oil and gas development conversation. We felt it was important that somebody from Dillingham participate in this workshop, to be seen and heard, to let everyone know we want to be part of the conversation in the future.

A View from Bristol Bay Borough, Alaska

Dan O'Hara, Mayor
Bristol Bay Borough, Naknek, Alaska

It is really nice to be here today. The mayors and council members are very close to what happens in our region, and we probably are tuned in to what goes on and the needs in our communities.

In the way of good news, gold hit $1,000 an ounce the other day. Oil is $116 a barrel, looking forward to $200—that should be fun.

The bad news is, the dollar has declined, and probably is the weakest in all of the world economy. The Japanese yen is certainly doing well. The headlines in the paper the other day said 900,000 homes are being repossessed in America, so I'm glad that Alaska's economy actually is much better than elsewhere. We're the richest state in the Union. Some of the people holding the money are tighter than two coats of paint, but we'll see if we can pry their fingers loose on some of that stuff.

Right now we're lacking quality in the Bristol Bay region. The Bristol Bay Borough was the first borough in the state of Alaska, and it is the sockeye capital of the world. But the economy in the villages is really interesting. Let me illustrate this.

I fly for PenAir. One day I had lunch with a pilot instructor, who asked me my opinion on the Pebble Mine. He answered for himself—he said, "I really am against the Pebble Mine." I said, "Do you have a recreation vessel in your household, and a four wheeler?" And he said, "Oh, yeah, I've got a skiff and an outboard motor, and two four wheelers." And I said, "You go on vacation? "Oh, yeah, I go on vacation every month." I said, "You're doing good. You must make about 125 to $130,000 a year and you're home every night. You can be against anything you want, you know!"

Now, let's follow that up with another part of the economy that we deal with every day. I walked into a home in a village, with a young husband and wife, five children. Very fine family, very meager income. The counter is plywood, the table is made out of plywood and 2 by 4s.

The floor is plywood. None of it is painted, and they have one couch and no TV.

Well, one day the young man was offered a job. He started working, and it isn't but a few months that he is actually one of the top guys in the drilling rig. I visited his house a year later, and guess what happened? He had a counter top. He actually remodeled the table. He put linoleum on the floor and they had a TV sitting in the corner. This is quite a change in just a year's time, with employment.

In our nearby communities schools are closing every year because people are leaving the village. In Egegik they have seven children in the school, and the village has a total of five jobs. There isn't anything wrong with moving from the village to Anchorage, but it really is difficult to move if you're forced into it because of the economy. That is exactly what we're faced with every day in our villages.

The fishing industry has been very difficult. In 1988 we got $2.40 a pound, and in the early 1990s we got 40 cents a pound. Can you imagine living with that kind of a decrease in your income? We're in a desperate situation. We aren't going to make it on just fishing anymore. If oil and gas development does happen in our region, maybe some jobs will come into the villages.

In Naknek, in the Bristol Bay Borough, we have an 8,500 foot runway with all the approach systems that Los Angeles has. In fact, in another couple of years we will do away with the ILS approach (instrument landing system); it will all be GPS. Another thing that is pretty good about the Bristol Bay Borough is that you can get into King Salmon almost every day of the year. Plus we have a dock that never goes dry. And 85% of the fish in the region, including Port Moller, are brought up to the Bristol Bay Borough and Nelson Lagoon, and come across our dock. We're adding an additional 200 feet to it, to a total of 400 feet. Northland Services conducts a lot of container shipping between Bethel, Naknek, and Unalaska, which is important to the economy. Our dock plays an important role.

If offshore development were to take place off Port Moller, probably families would move into the Naknek community. We may not have everything that these people need, but we do have things in our community that could be offered. We have an excellent school and good churches.

We support the others at this meeting who offer their communities. If we don't support each other, it's going to be a failure. The Aleutians East Borough, the Lake and Peninsula Borough, and the Bristol Bay Borough have partnered to take economic steps to better our region.

Should the oil and gas lease go through, probably in the next five years there will be some opportunities to go ahead and do some work. The Shell Oil Company came to our borough and told us the number of people they would hire for their platforms, and they told us the number of people they would need to do subcontracting work, and those numbers are huge.

The Southwest Alaska Vocational and Education Center in King Salmon is going to train 40 people in scaffolding construction. The second session will be electrical. And when those people finish with the training they will have a job. How often have you seen people get their 40 hour HAZWOPER training and their commercial driver's license, and then stand around for six months and not get a job, because they don't have the experience?

The mayors have their jobs cut out for them. It's going to take a lot of hard work, but we can do it. So, should offshore oil and gas development come, that will be fine. I signed a resolution supporting it, by the way, so you know exactly where I stand.

I appreciate the comments today that subsistence fishing is the number one priority, not sport, recreation, or commercial. One percent of the total salmon run is dedicated to subsistence by the State of Alaska, and I'm thankful for that.

In closing, a CEO for a corrosion-proofing company on the North Slope came to Naknek with the Shell Oil Company and others. A couple hundred village people came out. She was a very dynamic speaker. She said, "I want you people to understand that we are on a fast track if "OCS" ever does take place in Bristol Bay. The boat is leaving the harbor and you better get on it, because if you don't get on it one of these days your children will ask you—why didn't you get on that boat?" So that's why we're scrambling. And we want to at least be a little bit ahead should this thing ever come about.

Thank you very much. I appreciate the opportunity to talk with you today.

How Do You Balance the Value of Fishery Resources with Oil and Gas Development?

Stanley Mack, Mayor
Aleutians East Borough, Sand Point, Alaska

The Aleutians East Borough, located in the westernmost portion of the Alaska Peninsula, is a remote and ruggedly beautiful area. The Aleutians East Borough is pro-development, and supports oil and gas development **as long as commercial fishing and the subsistence lifestyle are protected**. I believe the two industries can thrive in our region, provided we proceed with care.

Commercial fishing has always been the driving force behind the five incorporated cities (Sand Point, King Cove, Akutan, False Pass, and Cold Bay) and one village (Nelson Lagoon) within the borough. During the 1980s, commercial fishing families in our region were making a good living. Fishermen received $2.85 per pound for sockeye salmon. They paid less than one dollar per gallon for fuel. However, we've seen a complete reversal of that trend in recent years, and it's taking a toll on families in our communities. During the summer of 2008, our fishermen received 70 cents per pound for salmon and paid $4.85 per gallon for fuel. Families are struggling to make ends meet. Young people are leaving their homes in pursuit of jobs elsewhere because of the lack of opportunities. As a result, the borough is seeking diversification to stem the tide of out-migration and provide residents with additional revenue and jobs.

A tentative offshore lease sale (Lease Sale 214) is scheduled for 2011, and offers the possibility of new jobs within the energy industry. Lease Sale 214 involves a wedge-shaped, 8,700 square mile area located in the North Aleutian Basin near Nelson Lagoon. Many of our borough's families may choose to remain within the fishing industry. Therefore, it's critical that commercial fisheries and subsistence lifestyles are protected. The borough is a cooperating agency, and is diligently working with the U.S. Department of the Interior Minerals Management Service

(MMS) to put together stringent mitigation measures that will protect the commercial fishing industry and subsistence way of life.

Fishery cycles

In addition to serving as mayor of the Aleutians East Borough, I am also a lifelong commercial fisherman. Commercial and subsistence fishing in this region is a tradition that is centuries old. For thousands of years, Aleut families have lived and subsisted here. My father came to this country in 1909 and moved to the island of Sanak, 42 miles southeast of King Cove. There he met my mother, an Aleut lady. They lived there until 1920, when the cod suddenly disappeared. They had to relocate where there were more opportunities, so they moved to King Cove where I was born. Salmon fishing was the only way to make a living then. When I was old enough to participate in family gatherings, everyone in my family of 18 had a job to do. We went salmon fishing in the summer. We would salt salmon so it would last us through the winter. Then we would hunt caribou, and salt and preserve the meat. During the spring, we gathered and preserved seagull eggs. It was a wonderful life. However, the ability to make a decent living within the fishing industry began to deteriorate.

As I was growing up, it was common to see some species disappear, only to be replaced by others. Throughout my childhood, there were no cod and very few halibut. In the 1970s, that began to change. The area surrounding Kodiak was beginning to produce some cod and pollock. We were so excited when we pulled the first cod out of the crab pot at Unimak Bight. Gradually, the quantity increased. Today, the cod stocks have peaked, and now we're witnessing a decline. Pollock stocks are also plummeting.

Oil and gas activity

In 1967, during the crab decline, we heard discussions about the possibility of a lease sale that would occur in the Bering Sea. The energy industry began conducting shore exploration along the mainland near Nelson Lagoon. At the time, Cold Bay was buzzing with activity. Then it shut down.

During the 1980s, St. George basin exploration activity ramped up. I watched the activity and the traffic it attracted. However, very little oil was found and the work there also shut down. Shortly afterward, oil and gas industry representatives contacted the Aleutians East Borough, indicating they were interested in exploring our region. As a result, we invited government officials and fishermen in from the Shetland Islands to share with us how the fisheries industry there has been able to coexist successfully with the energy industry.

Coexistence

Today, we in the Aleutians East Borough are faced with the same prospect. We have researched the advantages and disadvantages to opening up the North Aleutian Basin to oil and gas exploration. In 2005, we invited various groups to take part in a summit in Cold Bay. Participants included fishermen, residents from the North Slope, Prince William Sound and Cook Inlet, and government officials representing MMS, Alaska Department of Fish and Game, and U.S. Fish and Wildlife. As a result, we gathered a tremendous amount of information on how best to protect our economic base, the commercial fishing industry in our area, and our subsistence lifestyle.

In addition, we have traveled to other parts of the country and the world to visit oil platforms so we could learn about the latest technology and how renewable resources are protected elsewhere.

The last trip I made to Norway was very impressive and quite an eye-opener. We learned that Norwegian fishing communities have been able to successfully coexist with the energy industry by having a seat at the table during the initial discussions of development. The communities participated in negotiations with the oil and gas industry so that both sides would derive benefits from energy development in that part of the world. That is a valuable model for our borough to follow.

Our communities

We've discovered that preparing our residents and the younger generations for possible energy development in our region is key. This year, many of the young people from Sand Point, St. George, St. Paul, Unalaska, Dillingham, Igiugig, New Stuyahok, Perryville, Naknek, and Koliganek have taken part in a vocational training camp in King Salmon. As a result, they have been offered jobs on the North Slope. Similar job opportunities could be provided if oil and gas development occurs within the North Aleutian Basin in the near future. I believe we can work together with the Alaska Department of Fish and Game and the North Pacific Fishery Management Council so we can continue to protect one of the world's richest fisheries.

While some residents have moved away from the Aleutians East Borough due to a lack of opportunities, many fishermen and their families wish to remain in their communities where they have long-established roots. Despite the cyclical nature of the various fish species, it's clear that commercial fishing and the time-honored tradition of our subsistence lifestyle will remain. It's important to our borough residents, and we intend to protect that lifestyle at all costs.

During the past several years, the borough has built new infrastructure to support its fisheries. That infrastructure could also be used to support development of the oil and gas industry. We are doing our homework to protect the fisheries and have created a long list of mitigation measures that we are proposing, long before energy exploration can occur. Lessening the nation's dependence on foreign oil is also critical. I'm confident if it's done correctly, fishing and energy development can coexist in our region and provide a variety of new opportunities to benefit borough residents and the nation as a whole.

North Aleutian Basin Potentially Impacted Communities—Opportunities and Concerns: Audience Questions and Answers

STEPHANIE MADSEN: I think the message you heard today is that times have changed, they continue to change, and we need to change as well. I have full confidence that the leaders of our communities will lead us in the right direction. Let's give them a great round of applause.

MR. PLATNAKOFF: This question is for the Mayor of Unalaska. As you know, I lived out in Unalaska for six years and just moved to town. I was born and raised in the Pribilofs. I appreciate your report, and all that showed us what industry has done for the lifestyle of those who live and work out in Unalaska. I just wanted to point out that people's lives might be impacted negatively because of the developments that take place in Unalaska. In order to put in the new bridge to replace the existing one, a 3,000-year-old archeological site was dug up with a backhoe. How many remains were removed to put the bridge in while using this tactic?

MAYOR SHIRLEY MARQUARDT: Just very briefly, certainly development does cause changes in communities. This situation is a little different. The State came in and said the existing bridge that had been built almost 30 years ago was not engineered to handle many of the loads that we've seen in the last 20 years. It was sinking and unsafe. So they choose to replace the bridge and also sign the memorandum of agreement and understanding with both the Ounalashka Corporation and the Qawalangin Tribe through a one-on-one personal process.

I don't specifically know the number of remains removed, because that is information still forthcoming through the study, and will probably be released by the Ounalashka Corporation or the Qawalangin Tribe if they wish to make that public. They feel fairly private about the issue.

Q: You mentioned that you signed a resolution supporting OCS development. In what capacity was that—as the mayor of the borough or representing Bristol Bay Native Corporation?

MAYOR DAN O'HARA: Actually the resolution was passed before I became mayor. They revisited it again, and I signed it.

Q: Do you know the date on that?

MAYOR DAN O'HARA: Maybe a year and a half ago.

Panel

Native Culture and Subsistence Implications

Bristol Bay Native Corporation and Enrichment of the Native Way of Life

Tiel Smith, Lands and Resource Manager
Bristol Bay Native Corporation, Anchorage, Alaska

I was born and raised in Dillingham, Alaska, and I am a lifelong fisherman of Bristol Bay. Out of necessity and opportunity I live in the Anchorage area now, working for the corporate office of Bristol Bay Native Corporation as their lands and resources manager.

Daily I work closely with about 30 different villages within our Bristol Bay boundaries, on economic development projects. I work with them on their land conveyance and ultimate entitlement to their allotments and to their village corporation lands.

Bristol Bay Native Corporation has made a contribution to this week's dialogue. BBNC encourages and supports information sharing, especially around important resource issues such as those spoken about at this meeting.

What I want to highlight is subsistence. When it has to do with a regional corporation, subsistence has a unique twist. We are the subsurface owner to three million acres in a boundary of 34 million acres. So when you go to our Web page or look at our mission and vision you'll see "enriching our Native way of life." This presentation is about how the Bristol Bay Native Corporation helps our 8,000 shareholders enrich their Native way of life through their subsistence uses.

The late Harvey Samuelson, BBNC director and president, said, "The learning curve during the first decade was phenomenal: learn about the Act, learn about business (competition, financial statements, management), learn about corporations, choose a CEO, select land, pick investments, and communicate all this to the shareholders." This embodies what I think our early leaders felt and imagined as they started the Native corporations at the beginning of the Alaska Native Claims Settlement Act.

The Bristol Bay area in southwestern Alaska is about 150 miles from Anchorage. Its area is about 34 million acres or 40,000 square miles. At the inception of the Alaska Native Claims Settlement Act, the Bristol Bay Native Corporation was entitled to about three million acres of subsurface lands. The surface lands would ultimately go to the village corporation.

The different land classifications within this boundary are the conservation lands, state lands, Native lands, and federal lands. A large chunk of the lands are major parks and refuges—Wood Tikchik State Park (the largest state park system in the United States), Togiak National Wildlife Refuge, Katmai National Park and Preserve, Becharof National Wildlife Refuge, Alaska Peninsula National Wildlife Refuge, Aniakchak National Monument and Preserve, and Walrus Island State Game Sanctuary. I highlight these because as we consider our land management strategy we really do think about these lands and how they benefit all the stakeholders in the area, particularly our shareholders, and we manage our lands accordingly.

There are many attractions in the area: black sand beaches, mountain ranges, lowland tundra, wetlands, volcanoes, abundant flora and fauna, and wild and scenic rivers. Within the region are approximately 29 villages. They are made up of Yupik (Eskimo), Aleut, and Athabascan. Each has their own distinct Native language and dialect and their specific local arts and crafts.

Bristol Bay is known for its renown salmon runs—king, sockeye, silver, chum, and pinks, plus rainbow trout, arctic char, grayling, northern pike, lake trout, and Dolly Varden. Beluga whales and orca whales also follow the salmon runs.

A few of the native animals in the area that are used for subsistence are moose, bear, caribou, walrus, beaver, porcupine, otter, and fox. The highlighted activities within the region are wildlife viewing, boating and rafting, fishing, hunting, traditional subsistence activities, air tours, hiking, cannery and museum tours, and historic sites.

Regarding the economy, one of our main focuses in Bristol Bay is to assist in the lower cost of energy. Culturally speaking subsistence is the heart and soul of our region. Historically, commercial fishing is the economic mainstay. Government is the major employer whether it is federal, state, borough, city, or tribe. Tourism is a growing sector in the region. Construction is a constant activity in the region. Many capital improvement projects are government funded. To date the gravel sales for the Bristol Bay region on the Bristol Bay Native Corporation side equal about $10 million.

At the inception of the Bristol Bay Native Corporation, we were given $32 million and three million acres. We've done a lot of business and investments. A couple of highlights would be Peter Pan Seafoods, purchased in 1975 and sold in 1979 for a gain of $13 million; and the Hilton Hotel, purchased in 1977 and sold in 1997 for a gain of $46 million.

Current business activities include vertical and horizontal construction, engineering, oil field services, government contracting, environmental remediation, cardlock fueling, and information technology. The proceeds were used to pay dividends, increase the portfolio, and invest in new business operations.

BBNC has grown to a company with revenues of approximately $1 billion. Currently the investment portfolio totals approximately $100 million. Dividends have increased steadily since the inception of the Native corporation. Not all regional corporations can say that. The total dividends paid back to the shareholders since 1971 are $75 million.

The 7i provision revenues to date are $70 million from other regional corporations, half going to the regional corporation and half to the village corporations. An estimated $5 to $10 million will be received from 7i revenues in 2008. (Under the 7i revenue-sharing clause in ANCSA, 70% of the profits corporations receive from developing natural resources such as minerals, petroleum, or timber are divided among the 13 regional corporations based on shareholder enrollment.) Like our sister regional corporations, BBNC continues to assess regional natural resources, both renewable and nonrenewable. As a part of this effort we continue to educate ourselves and our shareholders through information sharing, and when possible first-hand tour experiences.

By resolution BBNC supports oil and gas exploration with an emphasis on the onshore. A key point is that we understand that if the offshore is not available to the industry, it is likely that they will not look at the onshore and therefore BBNC lands.

Most recently I traveled with Bristol Bay Native Corporation board member Russell Nelson and tribal leader Tommy Tilden to look at the coexistence of oil and gas development and fish on Sakhalin Island in Russia. Whether or not the Bristol Bay region is subject to a similar coexistent situation, it seems prudent to inform ourselves of similar circumpolar situations as we make decisions going forward.

BBNC has actively supported the education of its shareholders since inception. In 1992, we established a BBNC Education Foundation. Its current investment portfolio is approximately $3 million. There has been a significant growth in scholarship awards from the BBNC Education Foundation, totaling to 1,700 scholarships worth more than $1.4 million between 1986 and 2007.

BBNC has also established a shareholder management-training program called "Training Without Walls." We view much growth happening into the future and we look forward to Bristol Bay Native Corporation and its shareholders being a part of that.

Thank you for your time today. I'd like to thank Alaska Sea Grant and others for the opportunity to participate. Personally I would like to thank BBNC leaders and local corporation and tribal leaders for attending. I have benefited greatly from the dialogue that has happened so far.

Conservation in the North Aleutian Basin in Support of Subsistence

Norman N. Anderson, Fisherman
Bristol Bay, Alaska

I first of all need to show my appreciation to the Eklutna Natives for welcoming me onto their traditional lands. From the elders of the Bristol Bay region, I carry a welcome and best wishes.

I am the youngest son of Edward J. Anderson of Akutan, and Alma Christensen of Ugashik. I was born in Naknek, and lived there most of my life, I am a commercial fisherman as were my parents and are my sons. I was fortunate to be raised not just by two caring parents who lived off the land, but also many elders who taught me the respect of caring for our land and keeping our waters safe.

One elder who comes to mind, lovingly regarded by many as Gramma Nicolet, was Momma Nicolet to us who grew up in Naknek. Momma's traditional knowledge far exceeded what I learned at the territorial school in Naknek. She taught me about the stars and our planet Earth. She knew of the earth's "radiator"—how the exchanges of water cycle around the earth, and how each spring warm northward currents create ideal conditions for plankton, which then moves back south and feeds the incoming schools of herring and salmon. She told me any interruption in this cycle would be the beginning of the end for our way of life.

Forty years went by, and one day I was at a climate change gathering where I heard a speaker talk of the earth's climate and how the exchanges are at different times now. The water is warmer, and we see different species in the north. Humans are causing this change.

Now let's focus on our reason for being here today. The Minerals Management Service has Alaska divided into fourteen planning areas, seven of which are in the Bering Sea. OCS Sale 92, now called Lease Sale 214, is located off the coast of Nelson Lagoon. Seismic testing will precede actual exploration. Seismic is the practice of a series of repeated air blasts. Scows towing air-charged cylinders release these blasts, and longlines with receivers pick up the results of pictures from the ocean floor and what lies beneath. At this point human-generated sounds are going to tell the explorer where to drill.

Imagine an area that since the first Aleuts laid eyes on it has not ever heard anything louder then the last underwater volcano. Now the intent is to detonate thousands of blasts to see what's there, an area that seals, sea lions, walrus, sea otters, whales, salmon, herring, halibut, surface and subsurface clams, king crab, and millions of migrating sea-birds call home, not to mention the millions of organisms that each of the above depends on for food. Thousands of cannon-equivalent blasts are going to be created, next to and above all that live there and are just passing through. Work with me for a minute, but have you considered why in pet stores, on aquariums it says, please do not tap on the tanks?

Should oil and gas be found, we next will see the increase of vessel traffic on both sides of the Alaska Peninsula, producing more noise in a now relatively quiet area. Offshore rigs will be brought in, and drilling will soon start. Drilling mud containing arsenic, lead, and volatile chemicals will be spilled or dumped overboard into the path of fish.

To quote my friend Jay Hammond, "I cannot for the life of me think of a worse place to do something of this nature." This area is home to the endangered North Pacific right whale. What other species will join this list?

Sharing a common border of this sale area is "cod alley," where our CDQ fishery takes place. Another fishery that has brought this area into homes worldwide is the king crab fishery. Vessels I know such as the *Cornelius Marie*, the *Northwestern*, and the *Maverick* are involved in the world's "deadliest catch," made famous on the Discovery Channel.

I want to change lanes for a moment, and change your mental image of crab boats being slammed by high winds and waves pounding men to their knees. The *Selendang Ayu*, a Malaysian freighter filled with soy-beans, innocently passing south of this hazardous area, slammed her engines into neutral for tune-up. In the high seas the anchors could not hold this vessel and we all remember what happened next. The lives of six crewmen were lost. Soon the beaches of Unalaska and Dutch Harbor were littered with beans and a Coast Guard helicopter lay in a pile, a helicopter that would still be in operation saving lives of crabbers and others in the Bering Sea. Bunker oil that washed ashore stopped a resi-dent halibut fishery. Subsistence life halted, and traditional medicine picked off the beaches could no longer be gathered, all from one load of soybeans.

Should oil and gas be produced, run through a pipeline across the Alaska Peninsula to a tank farm, where crude will be pumped onto wait-ing tankers and then brought to refineries elsewhere? The trip out of Balboa Bay via tanker is no straight line, nor is it out of Valdez. It would take a couple of doglegs, in high winds and rough seas. Picture in your minds Valdez after the oil spill: the oil-laden waves, the dying sea otters, eagles and huge numbers of other seabirds, and a herring fishery that may never come back. Beaches prized for their clams, now abandoned for fear of contamination. Families ruined, lives jeopardized from inhaling contaminated air while attempting to clean soiled beaches.

My mother, bless her soul, called me the last nomadic Aleut. I travel to the lower Alaska Peninsula to gather with my relatives to hunt geese and dig for clams. I commercial fish and subsistence fish in Naknek, and I hunt in the Nushagak area where I now live. I trade food with relatives and friends, as this is the subsistence way. Our traditional food feeds not just our bodies, but is our way of sharing what the land and waters have to offer. Salmon, halibut, herring, and many other delicacies have for thousands of years given us strength. We Natives live for what is on the land and in the waters, not what lies beneath the land or under the water. Our capture does not harm what we gather, yet others destroy and make a profit. My lifetime take will not be noticed, and it will provide for my family and me. One accident of theirs will forever remove any chance for others to sustain.

An elder told me a story. I believe this happened back when Mt. Katmai erupted. He told of a time when the ground was covered with ash and it killed all the animals and fish. It was a time of famine; families got sick and many died. His memory brought tears to his eyes as he told the story of babies soon not even being able to cry. If we allow the mineral and hydrocarbon industry to destroy our land and water, we will see a time of famine, or government cheese. Mother Earth has a way of healing herself from her own destructive forces, but when man becomes involved, we lose.

Our subsistence and commercial fishery cannot speak for itself. Many Native voices will not be heard here today. I do not speak for them. I cannot speak for those elders who saw the value of our lands and sea; I can only repeat what the elder asked me, "Please don't let them hurt the land." We all must remember that without sound geology, we cannot have sound biology.

I want to thank you for listening, and to thank you for inviting me. Tonight look at the land and say thanks for allowing me one more day of providing me protection. And remember we must all do what we can to save this big village we call Earth.

Understanding Subsistence Fisheries in the North Aleutian Basin

James A. Fall, Statewide Program Manager
Alaska Department of Fish and Game,
Division of Subsistence, Anchorage, Alaska

Introduction

Alaska Statute 16.05.094 directs the Division of Subsistence of the Alaska Department of Fish and Game to collect and report information about "all aspects of the role of subsistence hunting and fishing" in the lives of Alaska residents. Since 1978, the division's social science research program has included over 30 projects in the Bristol Bay and Aleutian Islands areas. Many of these studies describe community patterns of subsistence uses and have been conducted through partnerships with regional organizations and tribal governments. The division also administers annual harvest monitoring programs for salmon and halibut. The following overview is based upon this research.

Subsistence fisheries as part of mixed economies

Of the approximately 43 communities in the North Aleutian Basin area, 22 have less than 100 people, and only two have populations that exceed 1,000. About two-thirds of the population was Alaska Native in 2000. Subsistence fishing activities in these rural Alaska communities take place within a "mixed economy" with subsistence and cash sectors. Of the two, the subsistence sector tends to be more reliable over time, with the cash sector providing more variable economic opportunities. The sectors can be mutually supportive; subsistence harvests require the purchase of equipment, supplies, and fuel.

Features of the subsistence sector the local economies of rural Alaska communities include the following.

- High levels of participation in subsistence activities. According to the division's systematic household surveys, virtually every household in the Bristol Bay and Aleutian Islands areas uses subsistence foods and participates in subsistence harvesting.

- High levels of subsistence harvests. As measured usable pounds, subsistence harvests in most communities of this area exceed 200 pounds per person per year, the approximate average purchase by Americans of meat, fish, and poultry in stores.

- Subsistence harvests are diverse, with many households using 15 to 20 or more different kinds of subsistence foods annually.

- The composition of subsistence harvests varies by community. For example, in 2004 the subsistence harvest of the Dena'ina Athabascan community of Nondalton was made up of 61% salmon and 23% moose and caribou; in contrast, in 1990, in the Aleut community of Akutan, salmon represented 26% of the harvest, marine fish (such as halibut and cod) were 28%, and marine mammals (harbor seals and sea lions) contributed 23%.

- There is widespread sharing of subsistence foods within these communities that ties families together in relationships of mutual support and obligation.

- Specialization in subsistence harvesting occurs in most communities, where about 30% of households harvest 70% of the wild foods and share with many others. Productive households tend to have jobs and the cash income that is necessary to subsistence fish and hunt.

- Subsistence fisheries include efficient harvest methods that have adapted over time.

- Subsistence activities follow a patterned seasonal round that is shaped by resource availability, processing conditions, and other economic activities.

- Subsistence fishing and hunting take place within traditional use areas that can be depicted on maps. It is important to document these areas over a long time span to reflect changes over time; a single year's data are inadequate to depict all important areas.

- Kinship relationships and traditional roles based on age and sex shape subsistence harvesting and processing.

- Traditional ecological knowledge informs decisions about subsistence harvesting and processing. In turn, subsistence activities provide a context for sharing traditional knowledge across generations and for young people to learn cultural values such as respectful treatment of fish, wildlife, plants, non-wasteful use, and generosity.

Features of the cash sector of local mixed economies in rural Alaska communities include the following.

- Seasonal employment. According to the division's surveys, most employed adults in these communities do not work year-round.

- Relatively low cash incomes. Data from the 2000 federal census show that per capita incomes in most communities of this area are below the state average.

- Higher costs for goods and services than are found in more populous areas of the state on the road system.

- There is uncertainty from year to year about the availability of jobs.

- Commercial fishing remains a major source of jobs and cash income.

- Cash earnings are invested in the subsistence sector, for equipment, fuel, and supplies.

Some myths about subsistence hunting, fishing, and gathering in Alaska

These findings about subsistence fishing, hunting, and gathering in rural Alaska communities help to dispel some "myths" about subsistence in Alaska. These myths include

- "Subsistence is a type of welfare system." In fact, subsistence is a viable sector of local economies. Indeed, many households with higher incomes provide much of the subsistence foods in rural Alaska.

- "Subsistence uses are disappearing and are being replaced by purchased foods and year-round jobs." In fact, subsistence foods are highly valued and people strive to maintain their subsistence way of life.

- "Subsistence activities use 'primitive' harvest methods and should be restricted to these." In fact, subsistence harvesters use efficient methods and are always adapting to increase efficiency and control costs.

- "Only Alaska Natives are involved in subsistence activities." In fact, in this area and throughout Alaska, many non–Alaska Native people harvest and use subsistence foods.

How might oil and gas development impact subsistence fisheries?

The effects of oil and gas development are uncertain, but some potential ways in which development in this area could affect subsistence activities include the following.

- Reduce resource abundance.

- Pollute resources and habitats.

- Create scheduling conflicts for harvesters who obtain jobs in oil and gas development and production.

- Displace harvesters from traditional areas.

- Create competition for fish and wildlife resource through demographic change.

- Provide sources of cash through jobs to invest in subsistence activities.

Conclusion

In summary, subsistence fishing in rural Alaska, including the communities of the Bristol Bay and Aleutian Islands areas, takes place in a mixed subsistence/cash economy. The subsistence sector is critical to the sustainability of these communities. Subsistence uses have key nutritional, economic, social, and cultural components. The future of subsistence fishing, hunting, and gathering depends upon healthy fish and wildlife populations and continued access to harvest areas.

For more information

- Go to the Division of Subsistence Web site at www.subsistence. adfg.state.ak.us.

- Consult the more than 300 reports in the division's Technical Paper Series, most of which are available online.

- Consult the division's Community Subsistence Information System, a compilation of demographic, subsistence use and harvest, and other economic information based on the division's systematic household surveys, also accessible at the division's Web site.

Subsistence Is Highly Valued

Tom Tilden, Tribal Chief
Curyung Tribal Council, Dillingham, Alaska

I am a subsistence user. I think a lot of people take subsistence for granted. They don't realize that subsistence living is a full time job. It's not something that you do on occasion. It's not something that you do on weekends, but it takes up all of your time.

I am one of 13 children in my family. I've lived a subsistence way of life all my life. My family decided to move from Ugashik to Dillingham because of education for the older children and also for me. Then in 1963 we moved from Dillingham because Dillingham was too big. It was a huge community of 400 people. We moved about 40 miles up the Nushagak River, where my parents felt comfortable living in a community of 50 people. When it hit 65 they thought it was too big, so they moved upriver where they were the only ones. In all of these places we lived a subsistence life.

As a young boy I was given to my grandma and she raised me. She told me that we were very rich because we had food on the table; that's what she instilled in me. She had seen epidemics and lack of food in her life. She moved to Bristol Bay because of the richness of the land. Richness to her was being able to feed herself.

My sleeping bag was not a sleeping bag, but actually a caribou skin. My blanket was a caribou blanket. I didn't wear shoes. I only wore mukluks up until the time I went to school. I couldn't wait to wear shoes, and once I wore them they were difficult to wear. They felt like I was walking with planks.

So I underwent a lot of change in my lifetime. I was schooled in Japan. I was schooled at the University of Alaska in Dillingham, but I believe that the best education I ever received was from my grandparents and my parents and the way I was brought up to live.

I remember back in 1963 as a young boy we ran out of food. The winter was long and cold and hard that year, with the majority of the temperatures down to 40 below zero. The ice was thick. We made steps in the ice down to the river so that we'd be able to draw water. As spring came the ice didn't melt fast enough for us to get down to our summer fish camps. We were still up there the first week of June, and we ran out of food. Our chief in the village told the young hunters to go get whatever kind of meat they could. So the best hunters went out and came back with moose, beaver, rabbit, and ptarmigan.

When our teacher at the school heard about the food shortage, she freaked out. She had me go outside and hang the flag upside down to show that there was an international emergency and we needed help. When I told my dad that, my dad was very angry. To prevent the teacher from doing that again, he cut the flag pole line off. He said, "There's nothing wrong with us. We are okay."

We survived because not only did the hunters go out, but the gatherers went out, too. The gatherers found patches of bare ground where they were able to pick up berries that survived the winter. They peeled the bark off of the little birch trees and we boiled it up. We got fresh greens from the springs and ate them. We cut the buds off of some of the trees and boiled them up with our meat and the fish that we caught, and we survived. We subsisted. There was no emergency, except in the minds of those who thought that we were suffering.

In 1992 the fish did not come back into Bristol Bay. The federal and state government were slow in reacting to the disaster, but the people knew how to subsist. The people knew how to live off the land until the government was able to catch up and bring us the aid that we needed. Our lifestyle, our culture, and our way of life saved us. And that's what's going to save us now and in the future. We cannot put that in jeopardy. Is it worth the risk, should be the question.

You must take a look at the people who are at the table today. Take a look at their corporations and what drives them. The oil industry is driven by profits and dividends and re-election. Take a look at municipal governments and boroughs; they are driven by taxing these corporations and these businesses. And then you take a look at the subsistence users. The subsistence users are driven by food.

There's a big difference between the risk levels of the players who are here. Who is going to suffer the most? Who can recover? Those are some of the questions that need to be asked. I hope that some of these questions do get asked and answered. As pointed out by some of the previous speakers, subsistence is about culture. It is about our lifestyle. It is about who we are.

During a subsistence battle in Juneau, one of the people who was fighting subsistence said, if we took away your subsistence you would still live. Father Michael Oleska got up and said, Yes, they probably will live, but culturally, spiritually they will die a slow death. That's what will happen to us. So ask the right questions, and demand the right answers. Ask who is more at risk. Thank you.

Keeping Our Culture Alive

Katherine McGlashan
Unalaska, Alaska

My Native name is Katrina, and my tribal name is Dances with Wolf. My great-grandfather is from Scotland, and my great-grandmother is from Attu. I grew up with four siblings in Akutan and Unalaska. I remember seal hunting with my father. I remember seining with my brothers and sisters for salmon in the summer, fishing for halibut, gathering sea eggs, and picking salmonberries and blueberries.

How do we keep our culture alive? Every summer for the past 10 years our tribe, the Qawalangin Tribe, with many other sponsors, hosts a culture camp for one week. We have children and mentors from the Aleutian Islands who come together and educate one another. In the camp children learn how to catch and fillet fish, to either dry or smoke. They learn how to dissect seals and use the intestines to sew and make kamleikas raincoats. They learn to make Aleut hats. They learn how to Aleut dance on the sandy beaches. They also learn about flora and fauna for medicinal purposes. They learn the Unangan language and to cook the traditional foods.

After the *Selendang Ayu* and the *Kuroshima* oil spills we have subsisted less. Our spots to subsist were contaminated so subsistence use is not as prominent as it used to be. We also lost a sportfishing camp, Volcano Bay, due to the *Selendang Ayu* oil spill.

Our Natives rely on subsistence use for health. Our ancestors have subsisted for over 9,000 years.

In closing the questions I have are, What would the subsistence implications be? What is at stake? And what would be impacted? My answer is "our lives." Qagaasakung (thank you).

Panel

Perspectives on Energy-Fisheries in Cook Inlet

Benefits from the Oil Industry on the Kenai Peninsula

John Williams, Mayor
Kenai Peninsula Borough, Soldotna, Alaska

I appreciate the opportunity to come before you and speak about oil history and the benefits that oil presented to us on the Kenai Peninsula.

I have been living on the Kenai Peninsula for 40 years. I have a very diverse and varied background that covers not only the oil industry, but also teaching and the fishing industry as both commercial fishermen and a sport fishermen. I served 18 years as Mayor of the City of Kenai, and I'm in my third year as Mayor of the Kenai Peninsula Borough.

The history of oil on the Kenai Peninsula goes back a long way, but 1957 led us into the development of oil as an industry and as an economic factor. I dare say that was the turning point toward statehood. I doubt Congress would have allowed statehood if we did not have a viable method to support ourselves.

In one of the other panels there was quite a bit of discussion about subsistence, and worries about what oil would do to subsistence, its lifestyles, and so forth. Let me just say that fishing on the Kenai Peninsula is a lifestyle.

I was in commercial fishing for seven years. I had 10 set net sites on Chisik Island, but was not all that successful. We watched the fish price fluctuate from 85 cents to $1.05 or $2.05 and back again. The fishing industry is relatively unstable in that respect, whereas the oil industry has brought stability into the economy on the Kenai Peninsula.

On the Kenai Peninsula we've got subsistence fishing, the personal use fishery, sportfishing, and commercial fishing both onshore and offshore. And we have the famous dip net fishery there as well, where Anchorage folks come down every summer.

Looking back over the years, I don't believe that oil has ever had a lasting detrimental effect on the fishing industry.

There have been many benefits from oil development on Cook Inlet. When I first moved to the Kenai area in 1968 about 10,000 people lived there, and we were not a developed area. Today about 53,000 people live on the Kenai Peninsula. In the summertime, we get around 75,000 people on the Peninsula. They come there to work in the oil industry, which picks up quite a bit in the summertime, and also in both sport and commercial fisheries.

As a result the Kenai Peninsula has grown in services and offerings for the people. The taxpayers of the Kenai Peninsula expect and do receive quite a few services. The Kenai Peninsula Borough's overall budget last year ran about $106 million, and that's not counting the Board of Education budget, which is about $121 million this year. We have 43 schools.

We also have two major hospitals that are supported by the tax base. The hospitals are owned by the borough. They were voted bonding capacity by the citizens and therefore are paid for by the tax base of the citizens. A great deal of that tax base comes from the oil industry, about $11 million. Without the oil industry, and the tax base, it's very doubtful that the population would be there. The support for our 43 schools and the Kenai River campus of the University of Alaska would probably not exist.

I spent 17 years with the University of Alaska teaching petroleum technology and process instrumentation. That leads me to another discussion about oil development and about work in the oil industry. A lot has been said about the advances in technology. We've come a long way with technology in the 40 years that we've been working oil in Cook Inlet.

In the late 1970s I attended the University of Texas Offshore Drilling School. We were then looking at advances in offshore drilling and advances in offshore technology that would someday be used in critical habitat areas of the world. Some of those studies and designs that we looked at went on to be incorporated in places like the North Sea and Sakhalin Island.

I've made five trips to the Sakhalin Island region looking at their oil industry. I am familiar with the technology in Cook Inlet, and with the advances that will undoubtedly be used in drilling in the offshore of the Arctic as well. We have come a tremendously long way in developing technologies for locked-in-place platforms, semi-submersibles and floaters, and "subsea completion" where everything rests on the ocean floor.

Interestingly enough, the area out in the North Aleutian Basin where we're talking about potential future drilling has a lot of the same attributes as Cook Inlet, such as water depth. One thing that the North Aleutian Basin lacks in the southern portion is the ice line. We do have ice in Cook Inlet, but ice has never caused a detrimental issue with oil.

We did have a mishap with one of the tankers several years ago. And a couple years ago we had another incident with a tanker. The tanker broke loose from its moorings, ran aground, and fortunately was recovered on the next high tide because of new technology, new developments and, of course, new laws. This tanker had a double hull.

About a month ago I visited the docks and welcomed to the Cook Inlet a brand new tanker built in Korea carrying 400,000 barrels of Russian crude to our refinery. It has the latest technology for recovery in case of total power failure. It even has a computerized system of 16 tensioning lines for docking, which are all monitored with tension sensors to determine loads on the ship.

I bring this up because the shipping industry responded in a major way to the tanker that broke loose during winter ice, by designing a system that could be used in the event of anything like that happening again. The industry responds very quickly to those issues.

Regarding the 400,000 barrels of Sakhalin crude brought to Alaska, imagine running Russian gasoline in your cars today. It shows you that we need to move ahead with an energy plan for Alaska and begin to think about our energy future.

In considering the development of oil and gas, it can be very positive for the citizens and their children who get good educations based on the salaries that their parents earn. And it's also beneficial to the government that serves the people, by providing a good solid, sustainable tax base that furnishes funding for schools, roads, hospital, service areas, senior citizen centers, swimming pools, and recreational centers.

It buys our ambulances and fire trucks, and it does all those things that we as citizens like to see being done by our government. I have appreciated the oil industry and I've appreciated the commercial fishing industry as well, all of these years. Thank you very much.

Cook Inlet Oil and Gas

Bill Popp, President and CEO
Anchorage Economic Development Corporation, Anchorage, Alaska

I'm going to give you a quick retrospective on the history of oil and gas in Cook Inlet, take a couple of quick snapshots of the past, and then look at it from a present perspective. And also I will look at it from the perspective of economics. I want to share this information with you as just a small piece of the equation, because there are a lot of issues involved in dealing with these different, disparate industries that have to try to work together when the oil and gas industry comes into a region.

The first discovery of crude oil in Cook Inlet was in the 1850s when Russian explorers recorded their first observations of oil seeps in the Iniskin Peninsula on the lower part of Cook Inlet. The first drilling attempt was on the Iniskin Peninsula in the early 1900s, and there were several additional attempts on that same area, all pretty much dry holes.

The first commercial discovery of crude oil in Cook Inlet was in 1957 at the Swanson River Field. Peak production for Cook Inlet was in 1970 at 83 million barrels that year. Oil production in 2006 was 6.1 million barrels. We've seen a dramatic drop in production, due in no small part to a major distraction known as the North Slope, which drew a lot of attention away from Cook Inlet.

Total oil production to date is 1.33 billion barrels. It's been a very significant amount of production, most used in-state. There has been some export of the oil, but for the most part it has been consumed in Alaska and the United States.

Natural gas production to date is 7.3 trillion cubic feet. There are about 1.6 trillion cubic feet in proven reserves. We used about 196 billion cubic feet in Cook Inlet in 2006, which powered about 80% of the electric grid. It also powered approximately 60% of the population for heating, so it's a very significant part of our energy picture in the Railbelt region of Alaska.

After many attempts, we hit oil in the Swanson River in 1957. This has often been credited as one of the key pieces to demonstrate to the federal government that Alaska could be economically viable as a state and is likely a key reason that we were able to get statehood in 1959. The early technology was not up to today's standards in health, safety, and environment, however.

We have not had a flawless process in developing oil and gas in Cook Inlet. After exploration was really starting to take off, a gas blowout took place offshore in the upper part of Cook Inlet in 1962. To deal with the situation they went ahead and lit it on fire. We had an eternal flame for a few months out in Cook Inlet until they were able to drill a relief well from the offshore drilling rig, relieve the pressure, and shut it down.

Three other very significant events in Cook Inlet included the 1987 Glacier Bay tanker spill, which spilled 159,000 gallons of crude oil. Then in 1987 we had a natural gas blowout at the Steelhead Platform, which burned down about half of the platform. Nobody was hurt, but it was a significant event. A blowback preventer failed on the natural gas drilling operation. And in 1989 the tank vessel *Exxon Valdez* ran aground in Prince William Sound and oil fouled the beaches in Lower Cook Inlet.

In Cook Inlet today, the newest platform is at the Redoubt Shoals. The Agrium facility, after 40 plus years of operation, just shut down and will not be reopening under any current plans that Agrium has announced.

On the west side, onshore development includes exploration for natural gas. One of our onshore drilling rigs is the Nabors 273 rig. The Marathon Glacier 1 rig is a very high tech piece of equipment that can mobilize from site to site in 48 to 72 hours, depending on how involved they are. It's a Mobile drilling rig.

In all, there are 16 platforms in Cook Inlet. Quite a bit of infrastructure in natural gas pipelines goes around the entire inlet, including crossing the ocean floor and running up the west side and east side of Cook Inlet into Anchorage. It serves the Matanuska Susitna Borough as well as the Municipality of Anchorage and the Kenai Peninsula.

There is also a significant liquids line on the west side that goes down to the Drift River facility. We have an oil collection station where the oil is shuttled across Cook Inlet by tanker over to the Tesoro docks.

To summarize the economic impacts to the Kenai Peninsula Borough, total revenues in 2005 were $83 million; $7.5 million of that came from the oil and gas property taxes and another $4.3 million came from the value-added facilities. Total estimated property taxes in 2003 were $47.8 million. We've seen a significant rise in the revenues to the Kenai Peninsula Borough in no small part from property taxes.

We had 1,389 oil and gas workers in 2005, about 18% of total Kenai Peninsula Borough total reported payrolls. The jobs in the oil and gas industry are very high paying, with an $80,000 average annual wage in 2004. The borough's average was $33,997 in 2004.

In 2007 there was a fairly significant resurgence in oil and gas employment in Alaska. The Kenai Peninsula Borough is starting to see some of that development in Cook Inlet. Out of 319,000 people employed in Alaska through the first three-quarters of 2007, 11,550 were employed in the oil and gas industry statewide with about 650 employed in the chemical manufacturing industry statewide.

In the Kenai Peninsula Borough, out of the 18,789 people employed, 969 were employed in the oil and gas industry and 335 were employed in the chemical manufacturing industry. That does not take into account the 150 or so workers who were laid off at the Agrium plant after its 40-year run. The average monthly wage in the Kenai Peninsula Borough for the first three-quarters of 2007 was $3,056. The oil and gas average wage for those three-quarters of 2007 was $9,885. It is a very significant part of our overall economy in the Kenai Peninsula Borough and in Cook Inlet.

Thank you for giving me this opportunity.

Cook Inlet Aquaculture Association

Gary Fandrei, Executive Director
Cook Inlet Aquaculture Association, Kenai, Alaska

Introduction

The goal and mission of the Cook Inlet Aquaculture Association is, through science and enhancement technology, to protect and provide the salmon resources of the Cook Inlet drainage. Our first objective is assuring habitat is protected; the second is that management has the proper tools and information available to make good decisions, and the third objective is to provide additional resources through hatchery production and other fishery enhancement techniques.

Similarities of the energy and commercial fishing industries in Cook Inlet

- Both industries harvest a natural resource.

- Both industries are highly regulated.

- Both industries are in the public eye.

- Both industries can be targeted by nonconsumptive advocates.

Issues between the energy and commercial fishing industries

There is a lack of open communication, particularly during the development of the energy resource. It would be helpful if natural resource user groups had a better understanding of where the industry thinks it might be going in developing oil, gas, and other energy resources. This would allow problems to be identified and resolutions to be worked out before significant financial and human resources are committed.

There is a need to address new issues or problems that arise once energy development proceeds. There is no system in place to address unforeseen issues that may come up from time to time. For example, tanker traffic in Cook Inlet and the recently established 1,000 yard exclusion zone has caused conflicts with the commercial drift net fishing fleet. It took over 1.5 years to resolve potential violations in Cook Inlet because there was no system in place in which to work out a solution.

There is a need for a system to identify common issues and to work cooperatively. Both industries need to take advantage of opportunities for partnering during the planning and implementation phases of energy resource development. Cannery Creek fish pass is a good example of what can be accomplished. The Cook Inlet Aquaculture Association and the energy industry worked together to identify a solution to a fish barrier, and have been working cooperatively to seasonally install and operate a fish ladder on the west side of Cook Inlet. There are likely more opportunities like this where both industries can realize some benefits.

Conclusion

The lack of good communication limits our ability to identify, understand, and find solutions to issues and problems that are critical to the success of both industries.

The Oil/Fisheries Group of Alaska

Stephen T. Grabacki, FP-C
GRAYSTAR Pacific Seafood, Ltd., Anchorage, Alaska

Peter T. Hanley[1]
BP Exploration (Alaska) Inc., Anchorage, Alaska

The Oil/Fisheries Group of Alaska was founded March 29, 1983, in anticipation of significant exploration and potential development in the Alaska outer continental shelf. The group had representatives of several major oil companies as well as major fishing organizations and processing companies.

The purpose of the Oil/Fisheries Group of Alaska was to provide a forum for inter-industry communication, education, and resolution of potential problems. The goal was successful coexistence of commercial fishing, processing, and oil industry activity. The objective was the formation of an open, easily accessible communication channel among group participants.

O/FGA bylaws recognized that the organization was to avoid and/or minimize offshore conflicts, not to be a forum to debate the issues related to offshore oil and gas development. The board of director positions were shared between oil and fishing industry representatives. For example, the president alternated annually.

The initial focus of O/FGA was geophysical activities. O/FGA's first product was *A Manual for Geophysical Operations in Fishing Areas of Alaska*, P.T. Hanley (ed.), 1984.

The publication contains fishing information:

- Fishing seasons and areas.

- Fishing gear, techniques, and vessels.

---

[1] Retired from BP Exploration, and past president of Oil/Fisheries Group of Alaska.

- Radio communications.

- Fishing industry contacts.

- Fisheries management and compensation.

- Charts of fishing areas.

- Drawings of fishing vessels and operations.

as well as geophysical information:

- Offshore geophysical operations.

- Geophysical vessels.

- Information sources for fishermen.

- Existing and future lease sale areas.

- Drawings of geophysical operations.

- Pictures of geophysical vessels.

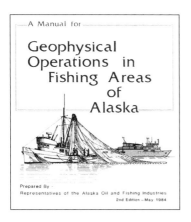

O/FGA also organized a symposium and a post–*Exxon Valdez* oil spill meeting. The group dissolved after seven years, as oil industry OCS activity declined.

Among lessons learned by O/FGA, for future Alaska exploration activity, are (1) encourage development of contacts and relationships between representatives of the two industries at all levels; (2) maintain a practical approach to avoid conflicts, not a forum to debate the merits of each industry's positions on resource development issues; and (3) provide mutual education on each industry's operations.

Cook Inlet Citizen Participation: The Keys to Success Are Collaboration and Broad-Based Participation

Michael Munger, Executive Director
Cook Inlet Regional Citizens Advisory Council, Anchorage, Alaska

An earlier panel discussed opportunities and concerns of citizens in potential oil and gas activities in areas of the Bering Sea. Although this panel is focused on fisheries and oil industry interactions in Cook Inlet, I would like to use my allotted time to tie this panel to that earlier panel by giving a brief overview of what we consider to be a successful mechanism for addressing stakeholder concerns regarding oil industry operations in Cook Inlet—and many of those concerns in our area have been fisheries related.

Background and introduction

The Cook Inlet RCAC was established under the Oil Pollution Act of 1990 (OPA 90) following the *Exxon Valdez* spill. OPA 90 established two RCACs—ours in Cook Inlet and one in Prince William Sound. Both RCACs were established under the premise that "only when local citizens are involved in the process will the trust develop what is necessary to change the present system from confrontation to consensus." The councils were intended to alleviate complacency, which many believe was a primary factor in the *Exxon Valdez* spill, by fostering long-term partnerships among industry, government, and the coastal communities of Alaska. To that end the mission of the Cook Inlet RCAC is "to represent the citizens of Cook Inlet in promoting environmentally safe marine transportation and oil facility operations in Cook Inlet." While there are many critical elements, I briefly want to discuss several of the most important aspects of Cook Inlet RCAC's approach: (1) collaboration with industry, government, and community partners; and (2) broad-based representation on the board of directors, or Council.

In doing so, I want to point out several major differences in our models and the potential development of similar models in your areas of concern. The Cook Inlet and Prince William Sound RCACs were formed many years after oil spill operations had been initiated in both areas. Cook Inlet has had active oil exploration and production since the 1960s and Prince William Sound since the 1970s. We inherited historical activities, existing regulations, and older infrastructures and technologies. We have been able to vastly improve the situations in each area through our efforts, improved technology, new regulations, etc. But you can build your process using our lessons, mistakes, and successes and can demand the newest and best technology and safeguards to be in place. I am not here to support or oppose development in the North Aleutian shelf areas. I am here to present what I believe have been the keys to successful citizen involvement in our area that could translate to your communities in the event that there is oil and gas exploration, development, or production activities.

Cook Inlet RCAC has often been described as a "watchdog" organization, but according to the intent of OPA 90 and our practices, the Council's role is to evaluate, advise, and recommend. Evaluation often means conducting our own scientific studies and advising and recommending means providing serious, thoughtful, and accurate input on many different issues. In that role, there are many times when not all parties agree and our recommendations and comments can be considered burdensome to industry or agencies. However, we have found that the biggest steps toward improving prevention and response measures in Cook Inlet, and the biggest leaps in improved regulations and safety improvements, have been those based on mutual respect, cooperation, and coordination among the citizens, agencies, and industry.

Examples of benefits and collaborative partnerships

By building collaborative teams, we have been able to access better information, garner greater financial resources, and work out conflicts early in the process. For example, we have worked closely with shippers and government agencies to identify potential places of refuge (PPOR) for stricken vessels. This project solicits input directly from local residents early in the process, instead of leaving the decision solely to regulators during an actual ship-in-distress event. A similar process was used to develop site-specific protection measures for especially sensitive areas—known as geographic response strategies (GRS)—allowing diverse stakeholders to identify the highest priority locations for protection in the event of an oil spill.

In addition to bringing citizen concerns to decision-making processes, Cook Inlet RCAC also communicates the efforts and perspectives of agencies and oil industry back to its broad constituency through citizen participation on the Council, as well as through other outreach efforts.

We have proven the benefits of our process of involving citizens during oil spill prevention and response planning activities and during actual oil spill response efforts in Cook Inlet. We have been able to provide better and quicker access to information, and have improved communications between Incident Commanders and local communities under stressful real-time events.

Thus we believe that one of the Council's greatest strengths is in its ability to find common goals and build partnerships between and among citizens, regulators, and industry while maintaining our ability to provide meaningful input toward change.

Broad-based representation on the Council

Broad-based representation in our organization is another key to the success of citizen involvement. Our constituency is diverse, and the composition of the 13-member Council or board of directors is designed to be as representative as possible of Cook Inlet's communities and various interests. OPA 90 built in a mechanism to ensure broad representation; we represent the Municipality of Anchorage, the Cities of Kenai, Homer, Seldovia, and Kodiak, and the Kenai Peninsula and Kodiak boroughs. Council members also represent specific interests, with one member for each of the following: Alaska Natives, recreation, environmental concerns, commercial fishing, aquaculture, and the Alaska State Chamber of Commerce. In addition to the Council members, nine nonvoting or ex-officio members represent state and federal government bodies with mandates related to oil industry operations and the environment of Cook Inlet.

Additional opportunities for citizen participation exist through public member seats on individual Cook Inlet RCAC committees. OPA 90 ensures representation by Council members and additional interested public members on each committee, ensuring that a wealth of information, expertise, and experiences is brought to the Environmental Monitoring Committee, and the Prevention, Response, Operations, and Safety Committee. Through these committees, many Cook Inlet communities and interest groups can be involved in efforts to promote safer oil transportation and production and minimizing environmental impacts.

We provide formal, legislated, organized, and funded mechanisms for multiple interest groups to raise concerns to companies and regulators early and often during all stages of activities, and our successes rely on our established and proven communication channels and relationships.

In conclusion

While I focused this discussion on the collaborative partnerships and broad-based representation on the Council that have been key to the success of our organization, there are other mechanisms for success. OPA 90 has identified numerous mandated tasks for both RCACs and we are meeting the identified goals through a combination of independent research, monitoring, and assessments; by obtaining independent scientific and technical peer reviews of our efforts; and through continued efforts in public outreach.

As I've stressed, our Council representatives provide the direct links between and among their constituent citizens, oil industry, and regulatory agencies. As well, our diverse staff develops and maintains relationships among these groups, ensuring that communications are up to date and even to the point of nagging and issuing demands when appropriate. Our most recent success story is that through clear and unanimous recommendations by our broad-based Council, and consistent communications by our staff, Tesoro recently committed to bearing the costs of placing a year-round assist tug for the docking of crude oil tankers at the Nikiski terminal—ahead of regulatory requirements.

That concludes my remarks. Thank you for your attention.

Cook Inlet Oil & Gas Development: Lessons Learned from 40 Years of Development in Offshore Alaska

Bob Shavelson, Executive Director
Cook Inletkeeper, Homer, Alaska

Cook Inletkeeper is a nonprofit organization that was started in 1995 by a group of Native folks, scientists, fishermen, and ordinary citizens, largely out of their concern with oil and gas impacts that they were seeing in the area.

Some people unfamiliar with us think that we received proceeds resulting from the *Exxon Valdez* oil spill. We did not. But where we did find some settlement money, for our start-up, was in the settlement of the Clean Water Act lawsuit that was brought in federal court against the major industry operators in Cook Inlet, including Unocal, Marathon, and Shell, for thousands of Clean Water Act violations. That's what got us started.

You've heard a little bit about the history of oil and gas in Cook Inlet. I want to focus more on the offshore area. To clarify, I don't mean offshore in the legal context; I mean in the water. Shell was the first company to install an offshore platform at Middle Ground Shoal in 1964, so they've got a long history in Cook Inlet.

Many benefits can come from oil and gas development. The industry has typically been looked at as a capital-intensive and relatively labor-poor industry, but the tax base that it supports and the jobs it supports are very important to the Kenai Peninsula Borough. Today I'm going to go through some of the public interest perspective—lessons that we've learned.

Lesson 1: Public dialogue means little if leasing and development are presumed

Before you ask how you're going to develop, you have to ask the question if you're going to develop. Governor Jay Hammond in 1977 answered that question in Kachemak Bay with a no. For those unfamiliar with it, Governor Bill Egan had improperly leased acreage in Kachemak Bay for offshore oil and gas development. Governor Hammond came in and recognized the vital importance of healthy fisheries to the communities in the area, and he bought back those leases for millions of dollars. He did a very important thing that should be a precedent for folks looking at Bristol Bay development. He created the state's first critical habitat area in Kachemak Bay, where surface entry for oil and gas development was made off-limits permanently. Of course the Alaska Legislature could go back and change its status, but I think with the growth of fishing and tourism in the area, that is unlikely in the near future.

We've seen a series of state and federal lease sale processes, and they really start to grind citizens down. They just keep coming back and coming back. People testify, and tell very personal stories about how oil and gas development is going to affect them and their tourism economy or their fishing economy. Overall, in response to citizens' concerns you might see some tweaking of the process, such as education measures. But the central thrust of the development moves forward, because it's presumed that we're going to develop.

A few years ago Minerals Management Service held a public hearing on Lease Sale 191 in Homer. It is unique because it represents a time when MMS did not go forward with a lease sale. When they came out with the announcement, people were excited about it, until we recognized why MMS didn't go forward with the lease sale. The lease sale did not go forward because there was low industry interest. Despite hundreds of people coming out and talking very passionately about their concerns with oil and gas, it wasn't the public interest that was heard, it was the industry interest that was heard. MMS spent millions of dollars on that lease sale, and they canceled it because there was low interest.

From our perspective, there is an inherent conflict built into MMS's mandate. Their first priority is always to lease and to drill, and the secondary mandate is to protect the environment and sustainable fisheries that it supports. There is tension, with the dual role that MMS plays.

Lesson 2: Government agencies often fall prey to industry pressure

The Clean Water Act lawsuit, in 1995, addressed thousands of Clean Water Act alleged violations. But in 2003 we had hundreds more violations at the same facilities. To the industry, paying fines simply becomes a cost of doing business. And paying fines is cheaper than compliance, so you continue to see violations.

When Congress passed the Clean Water Act in 1972 they envisioned a process where every five years a permit would be issued and technology would improve. The controls would be ratcheted down until eventually there would be zero discharge. But it has not worked that way.

In 2007 EPA issued an NPDES (National Pollutant Discharge Elimination System) permit in Cook Inlet that nearly tripled the amount of toxic heavy metals, oil, and grease that can be discharged into the public fisheries in Cook Inlet. In 2006 we had put out a report (Dishonorable Discharges: How to Shift Cook Inlet's Offshore Oil & Gas Operations to Zero Discharge) that showed that it's technologically feasible to re-inject the wastes rather than using our fisheries as a dumping ground. With oil now over $100 a barrel, Chevron, the primary operator in Cook Inlet, reaped $18 billion in profits in 2007. We think the right thing to do is re-inject these wastes, but EPA sided with industry and they issued the NPDES permit.

In 2007 we were forced to join hands with the fishing industry, including the largest drift net association in Cook Inlet, United Cook Inlet Drift Association, two Native tribes, and another fishing group to sue EPA. These lawsuits take a lot of time and money, and we feel that it's absolutely unnecessary for us to be there. One of the important things to recognize is that you can get into the cause and effect cycle, asking is there harm from these discharges or not.

Aside from those issues, a very important aspect relates to seafood marketing and marketing perception. Last night I was in a restaurant and an item on the menu jumped out at me, "Kenai Wild." We're branding and marketing our fish very successfully to combat this glut of farm-raised fish on world markets. Any perception that smudges the brand is not good for the fishing industry. So when toxic wastes are discharged into Cook Inlet, that's of concern. I think if you start poking holes in the fisheries in Bristol Bay you're going to find similar concerns.

Lesson 3: Oil and gas corporations will pass off (externalize) costs and risks to the degree they can

Corporations have one overriding fiduciary duty, and that is to maximize their profits for their shareholders. We could say that corporations are "externalization machines." They want to push the costs off to everybody else so they can maximize their profit. A classic example is the dumping in Cook Inlet; it's cheaper to use our public water resources as a private subsidy, as a dumping ground, than to properly treat and re-inject the waste.

In February 2006 the tanker *Seabulk Pride* was grounded at Nikiski, with five million gallons of product on it. Freeing the *Seabulk Pride* was a remarkable response, and they got it off the beach without a major incident. In response to the grounding, Tesoro bought a tug to assist ships at Nikiski, and we applaud Tesoro for that.

But for many years we had been saying that Nikiski was an inherently unsafe place to operate tanker vessels, particularly in the winter. A study was done in 1993 by Captain Dickson of Sullom Voe in the Shetland Islands. As a navigational safety expert in the North Sea gas fields, he made the recommendation that a tug was needed for docking and assists in Nikiski. Industry continued to put it off until the *Seabulk Pride* was grounded. That got everybody's attention.

In Cook Inlet we have more than 1,000 miles of oil and gas pipelines, and there are problems with the pipelines. We produced a report in 2002 which showed that there was about one spill per month and that on average about 50,000 gallons of oil was spilled per year. (A couple of large spills skewed the average.) It was not until we wrote the report and elevated negative public relations on this issue that there was some action on this.

What is the role of government in these things? We understand what corporations do; that's very predictable behavior. But we expect our government to play an objective, neutral arbitrator role. Instead, increasingly we're seeing that agencies at the state and federal level are getting "captured" by industry. We need more oversight on some of our extractive industries.

Lesson 4: The risks of transportation extend far beyond the area of production

The *Exxon Valdez* oil spill is the classic example of transportation risk. And we have other issues as well. Kachemak Bay is a port of refuge for stricken vessels. Damaged, leaking tankers have come into Kachemak Bay, a critical habitat area. In addition, ballast water discharges bring in invasive species. Smithsonian Institution scientists found about a dozen invasive species in the Homer harbor several years ago.

Lesson 5: Oil and gas resources are finite

The Agrium fertilizer plant in Kenai at one time had upwards of 300 employees, and now it is closed because of a shortage of natural gas. The oil and gas industry provides an incredible resource for the tax base on the Kenai Peninsula, but we knew the day that facility opened that it was tied to a finite resource, that it was going to close some day. As a result of the 2007 closure there are severe dislocations in the Kenai Peninsula Borough now, and people are looking for work. It is very disruptive.

The other side of the coin is that industry typically leaves a toxic legacy in terms of contaminated sites. The Kenai Peninsula is littered with hundreds of contaminated sites. These are documented in the

Alaska Department of Environmental Conservation's contaminated sites database. The Chevron 5 refinery near the beach in Nikiski is close to set net fishing sites. There is continual seepage of contaminated material from the refinery. It should be excavated and properly cleaned up.

I appreciate the opportunity to speak here today. Thank you.

Perspectives on Energy-Fisheries in Cook Inlet: Audience Questions and Answers

Q: I have a question for Mr. Munger. Can additional regional citizens advisory councils be formed, aside from the Oil Pollution Act (OPA)?

MICHAEL MUNGER: Yes, you can do that outside of the OPA 90 legislation.

GORDON SLADE: I'm interested in the oil spill protection resources in Cook Inlet. I'm from Newfoundland on the East Coast and we're looking at that whole situation today as our industry ramps up for more offshore production.

MICHAEL MUNGER: What we have in Cook Inlet are oil spill co-ops, where oil companies operating in that area share common costs for oil spill clean-up activities. We have the Cook Inlet Spill Response and Prevention Incorporated.

NORMAN ANDERSON: What percent of the fish are harvested once they pass Cook Inlet offshore rigs?

GARY FANDREI: Most of the oil industry platforms are located in the upper end of Cook Inlet. Most of the harvest of the adults would occur prior to the oil platforms. Pretty much all the smolt are going to pass those platforms.

BILL POPP: I want to offer one other perspective to keep in mind. Comparing Cook Inlet's technology today in terms of the number of platforms is not a fair comparison to what we would be seeing in any offshore development anywhere in the world right now. There are so many platforms in Cook Inlet because they're old and don't have the reach that new platforms do. Where you may have had four or five platforms on a given field, today you'll have one.

Commercial fishermen in the upper Cook Inlet are concerned about the exclusion zones that are mandated by the Coast Guard around platforms. They're worried about a loss of fishing grounds. That's a legitimate concern.

MAYOR JOHN WILLIAMS: Another thing that's different about Cook Inlet as compared to Bristol Bay, of course, is the tides. We have tides that are as high as 34 feet here at the dock in Anchorage. Down around the platforms those tides run as high as 27 feet, so you have a continuous washing back and forth in Cook Inlet, which would carry a large number of fish.

BOB SHAVELSON: The surest way to avoid conflict with commercial fisheries is to not have rigs in the water. Bill mentioned the technology improvements in the lower Kenai Peninsula Pioneer Resources and the region just north of Anchor Point. They've got a well where they've drilled out directionally from onshore and they're reaching federal leases out past three miles. We've really applauded that because it keeps the infrastructure onshore.

BILL POPP: Just to add to that, if the resource is 15 or 20 miles offshore, you're not going to be able to develop it for onshore. The reach is not there yet.

DAVE HARBOUR: It seems to me that two basic ways of approaching the problem have developed in this workshop. The first is to debate whether or not there should be a lease sale. The second approach is to assume that fishing and energy industries could identify and seek solutions to problems through collaboration. Could you comment on those two approaches?

MAYOR JOHN WILLIAMS: I think that over the last four years there's been a concentrated effort by both the oil and gas industry and fisheries to work together.

The issue of whether or not there should be a lease sale—that's a really interesting question. Let's see, oil was at $112 this week. I'm paying $3.59 a gallon in Kenai. Until the United States and the world decide they want to convert to something other than oil for energy, I think we're going to have to answer that question positively. Yes, we're going to have to explore. We're going to have to explore farther, deeper, and more broadly across the entire world in order to find those resources that we need to run our industry and continue to operate our society in the manner to which we've all become accustomed.

BILL POPP: I'm going to take a little different perspective on that than the Mayor did, before Bob responds to the Mayor. I've come into these sessions and I've done sessions like this in any number of different forums. I've had the privilege of having been invited to speak in a number of communities in British Columbia about the concept of opening up the Queen Charlotte Basin to offshore development. There is a huge can of worms in terms of all the different interests that are down there in a region, which is incredibly lush and beautiful and relatively pristine if you ignore the untreated sewage going into the water from a number of communities along the coast.

I'm not going to stand up here and tell anybody from the Aleutian Basin region or the Bristol Bay region that you should do this. You have your communities in some cases drying up and blowing away. Your citizens are moving out of your communities because of, ironically enough, the cost of energy. You've got the opportunity, perhaps, through this development to address those issues, but is that a good trade-off? Those are the things that your communities have to balance in looking at how you're going to afford and deal with this.

Trust me. I will tell you forthrightly that oil and gas development comes with baggage. The question is how do you address that? How do you mitigate it and at what level is it acceptable?

The Agrium closure did not create wholesale displacement in the economy of the Kenai Peninsula Borough. Most of the workforce got snatched up by the oil and gas industry because they were short on workers. There's a very small percentage left that have not been placed. Agrium may come back. The facility may reopen if a new gas supply is found. There are still opportunities for several trillion cubic feet of gas to be found in Cook Inlet. There may be an opportunity for North Slope gas to come to Cook Inlet. Maybe the facility will open, but you can't guarantee that.

You've got to look at these facilities when they come as opportunities to take advantage of. However, they are finite opportunities and that's where proper planning and forward thinking comes into play if this is what you want to see happen in your region.

BOB SHAVELSON: The gorilla in the room on this issue is climate change, which really hasn't been discussed at all here. We could drill every single drop of oil from the Alaska outer continental shelf and we wouldn't even begin to put a dent in U.S. demand. President Bush acknowledged our addiction to oil, which is fairly remarkable. I think we have to act on that and we have to act quickly because climate change is real.

Audience Decides on Next Steps: Discussion

BRIAN ALLEE: Now we have an opportunity to have an open forum to get input, ideas, and suggestions from the audience. We have a number of panelists in the audience who are willing to answer questions. We've heard some concerns from different groups as to what we're trying to do here. We're trying to create a dialogue and an opportunity to discuss issues. There are no foregone conclusions; the intent is to have an interesting, non-advocacy discussion of the issues of energy and fisheries in the North Aleutian Basin.

What does the group feel about concerns and needs that are not being addressed? We'd really like you to give one final push of energy, and state your opinion.

BOB JUETTNER: I'm with the Aleutians East Borough. I think this workshop turned out quite well. I have suggestions for improving it. One, I think we need to go forward with more discussion in the future. I thought we rushed through some scientific areas, such as seismic. A lot of questions about seismic went unanswered. I think we should continue with another workshop in the future, but focus more on the hard science—facts and figures. Jim Fall did a presentation on subsistence, which I thought was very good.

There are a lot of different regulations in this program.

I think it would be important to have more people involved. Maybe you could involve the Minerals Management Service (MMS) people who actually regulate what happens in the ocean, the Coast Guard, and the Environmental Protection Agency (EPA). I'd like to see small groups get together over the next year or so. We could reconvene in a year and maybe there would be a little more consensus.

MEL BROWN: I retired from BP after working for them for 30 years. I would like to see a panel of oil experts answer questions about selling the idea of safety for offshore platforms, describing the best success that Cook Inlet has had over the years. Also, some of the platforms out in the Gulf of Mexico have experienced some success in terms of the very dangerous weather conditions. It would be nice to give a pictorial of what subsurface valves do on screen. You could also show how the surface valves go into a shutdown process when an emergency like this comes up, because the technology has moved a long way in this particular area.

I worked for 16 years up on the North Slope at the first offshore facility, and we had some emergency concerns and went into a shutdown. We never experienced any spills during the years that I was up there. The technology has to be shown to the people, because if the North Aleutian Basin is developed it will be an offshore facility. I'd also like to see some information given in terms of training and job opportunities. I think this area needs to be discussed more.

I attended one of Shell's sessions last year, and they shared some preliminary development plans. It gave us an idea of how many platforms might be planned. Finally, is there enough seismic information to go on for the lease in 2011? Does the seismic take place after the lease sale?

GREGG NADY: Those are really good comments. At Shell, we're actually thinking about producing a video that would walk through the technology from the start of the seismic exploration all the way through development, production, the valves, and the shutdowns systems, etc. A video like that could be broadly disseminated. You make a great point, because we have to get more information out to people to make a decision.

Historically, we've developed many gas and oil fields with two-dimensional seismic so that's clearly an opportunity. New seismic is now with water, and I think MMS is considering that. They would have to do some environmental assessment before they could authorize it, so the likely scenario is that there would not be any new seismic before a lease sale.

JOHN GOLL: I'm from MMS. Yesterday I showed the seismic that was available. First of all, we've told companies that if anybody wants to come in and shoot seismic it's very likely we will have to do an Environmental Impact Statement (EIS), which is a major amount of work. The companies that we've been talking to say that, for the purposes of a lease sale, they probably would not need it. Some of the seismic companies are reprocessing the data, so the push to get out there before the sale may not be there. But before somebody would want to drill a well, they would have to do some search over the area. Part of the reason more seismic would be needed is to figure out where to drill the minimum number of wells. The seismic information collected today is 3-D. It has another benefit in reducing the number of wells that would have to be drilled.

MAYOR DAN O'HARA: I'm mayor of the Bristol Bay Borough. Should we start thinking about the permitting process? Maybe we could provide some input as to what we would like in the permit. Could we request this from MMS?

What's the purpose of supporting oil companies if we're not going to reduce our own energy cost and cost of living? Are we going to be able to get a reduced cost of diesel fuel coming to Bristol Bay?

I give you credit, Gregg, for coming here and talking with us because it's certainly been educational. If we meet in a forum again, I'd like to know what the oil companies are looking for in the way of subcontractors. Everything is happening on our lands and under our jurisdiction, so I think that's very important.

TOM TILDEN: I am from the Curyung Tribe. I suggest that someone from the Bristol Bay Native Association should sit on the steering committee, because the people of Bristol Bay are going to be impacted by the North Aleutian Basin sale. When you look at the environmental disasters that have happened, not only here but also around the world, like the *Exxon Valdez* oil spill, the *Ocean Ranger*, and the Alyeska pipeline, you find that the science was probably there. However, human errors caused those disasters. We really need to proceed with caution.

And I think that in addition to the Bristol Bay Native Association, you should also have subsistence users on the steering committee, because although there was a lot of emphasis put on fisheries today, that's not all that will be impacted. We haven't discussed seals, sea lions, belugas and other whales, clams, seaweed, and all the plants that are in the water and on the shoreline that the people gather every summer to live on. When I read the scientific material I can see that there is a lot of information lacking, and the only way to get that information is to expand the steering committee to include Native groups.

MAYOR STANLEY MACK: I am mayor of the Aleutians East Borough. I thought this was a very informative gathering. The one thing that was not shared is that there's a tremendous amount of traffic going through Unimak, called the great circle route. How are we going to secure that area when activity is going on? There's also a tremendous amount of activity in the Bering Sea. Plenty of folks don't realize how much oil is being spilled out there now, and there will be more. If there will be more activity, there should be a response vessel that is immediately ready to be dispatched.

TERRY HOEFFERLE: I'm from Dillingham. This gentleman asked a good question and I'm not sure that he got a good answer. He talked about the importance of asking the question, should an oil lease sale happen in Bristol Bay.

Curyung Tribal Council chief Tom Tilden talked about some of the other nations that are involved in this decision and the migratory birds all along the coast of Western Alaska and northwest Alaska that stage in that area. I'm haunted by comments made by MMS that there will be a major oil spill during the exploration and development of the field in this lease sale area. I'm haunted by the fact that folks who are involved in oil spill clean-up work say there's not a boom that's made anywhere that can contain an oil spill in seas of more than three meters.

I think that the conference today presupposes that a decision has been made to have an oil lease sale in this area. I'm not entirely convinced that the issue has been thought through and debated. I would welcome the opportunity to have more meetings like this to talk with folks from the areas around Nelson Lagoon, King Cove, and Sand Point.

I come from an area that was the subject of major industrial extraction 50 years ago, and the places are ghost towns now. If this project happens in a 25-year cycle, where are the jobs going to be at the end of 25 years? We will be at the same place, perhaps with less ability to rely on natural resources than we have today.

I would like to see a similar conference that would address whether we have the information necessary to make good decisions. I think there are people in the northern part of Bristol Bay who feel we are the risk bearers rather than the stakeholders. And that because of currents and atmospheric conditions, if there were a spill our estuaries would be in jeopardy and, unlike the folks who are near the resource area, perhaps some of the benefits to our local governments would not be there.

BRIAN ALLEE: Expanding the dialogue further by having more meetings is a good idea. Would you want to have more meetings in Anchorage or would you prefer to have meetings in coastal communities that are directly affected by oil and gas development?

TERRY HOEFFERLE: I would welcome the opportunity to talk about these things in Sand Point, Dillingham, or other places. It would be good for some of the scientists to come to Bristol Bay to see our 23 foot tides twice a day and see the spring tide or the fall tide and note the direction of the winds and the currents when we have a fall storm surge.

GORDON SLADE: I'm with One Ocean, Canada. I'm very pleased to be here today to listen to the dialogue. We didn't have the opportunity to have a dialogue like this in Newfoundland and Labrador in the 1970s and 1980s. The government said we were going to have oil and gas, and we got oil and gas. So what you've been doing here for the last two days is a very important exercise.

We've had oil and gas now for 10 years. The fishing industry and the oil and gas industry in Newfoundland and Labrador are working well together through One Ocean. They have good dialogue with the regulator, the Department of Fisheries and Oceans, but every day they have to be on top of things and think about possibilities. The fishers and the communities also have to be aware of what's happening. This information exchange is critical and it has to go beyond the capital city.

In our case at St. Johns, the information exchange has to be out in the communities. There are 604 coastal communities in Newfoundland, and you could ask these coastal communities how they are benefiting from the oil and gas. Of course they're not all affected. St. Johns is affected, and there are probably three places in the St. Johns area in Newfoundland that get a direct impact from oil and gas.

In the other communities, of course, as the government gets the revenue from oil and gas it can provide a better infrastructure so there are better hospitals, roads, etc. Generally, that's the benefit we see if you're living in Bonavista, St. Anthony, or on the coast of Labrador.

Since the Confederation of Canada, Newfoundland has always been the poorest province. In the past 10 years, oil and gas has enabled Newfoundland to improve public infrastructure comparable to other parts of Canada. So there is a benefit from oil and gas drilling, but people have to be informed and involved which is what you're doing here today. I would encourage you to have more of these sessions out in the coastal communities. I'm glad I was invited to come here today and I certainly wish you well in your deliberations.

Q: I've listened to much of the proceedings and I'd like to state that if we can have these kinds of meetings in the communities of Cold Bay, Dutch Harbor, or Sand Point, and look at working with all communities in the affected area, we can make an evaluation for ourselves regarding the actual impact of oil and gas.

I've looked at some of the options regarding the transportation corridors for possible gas and oil lines from the Bristol Bay side of the peninsula to the Pacific side of the peninsula. There has been a lot of satellite imagery developed for the Cold Bay area, around Izembek. Also, a lot of information has been gathered on the Lefthand Bay area and Sand Point shipping corridors.

When you start looking at the land base that is needed for the development of basic infrastructure to move oil and gas you realize you need a big footprint. And not to say anything against Cold Bay, but it does not have much of an area to fully develop a shipping facility. Cold Bay is boxed in by Izembek, which is currently embroiled in an environmental dispute about a road being created from King Cove to Cold Bay. You can imagine the kind of discussions and arguments that will occur, over developing the oil and gas facilities that would have to run through the heart of Izembek.

I think that the regional corporations, particularly the Bristol Bay Native Corporation and the Aleut Corporation, along with the Lake and Peninsula Borough and the Aleutians East Borough, need to sit down and find out exactly what they've got to work with and make demands now on the oil and gas industry.

I personally think that the oil and gas within the area are going to be developed. I think that is apparent, especially when you're looking at the geophysical problems that are blooming worldwide. I think we need to invite individuals from the State Department who would be willing to talk frankly with the residents within these areas to explore how serious the issue is regarding the development of energy resources within this country. That's imperative.

Regarding transportation infrastructure, I think the state administration needs to lay the groundwork for access across state lands on the Alaska Peninsula. The coastal plains of the Alaska Peninsula fall within state selections for the most part. The Department of the Interior needs to evaluate the necessity of crossing wildlife refuge lands. These lands belong to the people who live there. They should not be used as arguments to box in communities or to prevent local development.

There should be no problem regarding simple construction of a road from King Cove to Cold Bay. That argument should never have occurred. Those arguments will crop up again and again until the whole issue regarding access across the refuge lands is settled. Also, the presidential administration needs to be involved in the discussion regarding oil and gas development within Bristol Bay, not just MMS.

MAYOR SHIRLEY MARQUARDT: I am mayor of Unalaska. I think King Cove and Sand Point are going to be affected; they will be the communities that see the intense growth that Unalaska has already experienced. I think it's really important to bring this information out to the communities and certainly Unalaska would welcome any group that would like to come out.

PAUL STANG: I'm from Stang Consulting. I think you need to continue discussion here in Anchorage and also in the villages. I think the topics for future discussions will be clear in the proceedings of this conference, which will be published by Alaska Sea Grant.

Timing of future meetings is critical. MMS has a proposed lease sale schedule that they're going to pursue and that is about a two-and-a-half year process.

To answer Gordon Slade's question, the leasing decision has not been made. In fact, the purpose of the 1978 amendments to the Outer Continental Shelf Lands Act was to specify an analysis and decision process that would be presented to the Secretary of the Interior to decide whether or not the sale should proceed. Is there enough information? Well, under the National Environmental Policy Act (NEPA) you are to use the best information available to you. The difficulty is that if you wait until you have all the information that's possible to gather, then nothing would ever occur because you can never get to that point. That's one of the purposes of MMS's Environmental Studies Program, which to has spent $800 million gathering information in Alaska.

I think that the OCS Lands Act process is designed to get information out and the more this group can supplement the normal MMS process, the better. I'm almost certain that MMS will schedule public hearings in the communities along the Aleutian chain.

Q: I work with Pacific Environment and I attended some of those MMS scoping meetings. The one scheduled for Dutch Harbor, the nation's largest fishing port, was announced after the meeting occurred, which makes it a little difficult for people to give input.

When this conference was first brought up to me, I was told that it would be a conference about how to develop Bristol Bay oil and gas resources properly. The problem with the OCS Lands Act is that it's not about doing it properly, it's about getting oil out of the ground and that is what this is focused on.

Regarding ocean policy in the United States, we had a couple of blue ribbon panels examine how the United States has treated its ocean resources over the past five to ten years. This blue ribbon panel said we don't do a very good job of it. We have a hodgepodge of laws and agencies that all try to work together, but there is no uniform work being done. There is no multiple-use zoning that's undertaken before activities are planned. Also, there's also no real ecosystem-based management.

I think the Norwegian Integrated Management Plan is an important example for us to look at before we undertake drilling. The recommendations of the U.S. Commission on Ocean Policy should be considered as well.

Under the Norwegian Integrated Management Plan, would you drill in the heart of fisheries habitat and in the heart of the designated critical habitat of the world's most endangered whale population? I think that's the question that should be asked.

Would you put drilling rigs in endangered habitat, and run subsea pipelines through eider habitat and over land through more endangered eider habitat to an LNG (liquefied natural gas) terminal, which would be sited right in the critical habitat for endangered Steller sea lions? I don't think these questions have been answered.

If the North Pacific Fishery Management Council can spend so much time working to protect an area like Bristol Bay because it's so important to the $2 billion fishery, if the International Pacific Halibut Commission can close the area to halibut fishing, if the Council can close the area to bottom trawling, why are we considering opening these areas to oil and gas development? It just doesn't make sense to me and I think we have to step back and ask these broader questions. Thanks.

GRAHAM LONG: I'm from Compass Resource Management. I'm following up on the discussion we had about trade-offs. Over the last two days, we've talked mostly of the positives and generally of the downsides, which tend to be more complex. Going forward, we need to reduce ambiguity in our questions. That's the biggest challenge right now.

BRIAN ALLEE: Thank you. This meeting was not about presupposing any sort of development. It was about a dialogue from the outset. Denis Wiesenburg, Dean of the School of Fisheries and Ocean Sciences at the University of Alaska Fairbanks, and I are going to look at these questions and we will consider follow-up meetings. So don't hesitate to provide input. Most PowerPoints from this meeting will be on Alaska Sea Grant's Web site (http://seagrant.uaf.edu/conferences/2008/energy-fisheries/agenda.html). We will also publish a proceedings book. Again, I very much appreciate your participation. Thanks.

Index

Bold page numbers indicate figures, tables, and map